The workpLace revoLution

Restoring Trust in Business and Bringing Meaning to Our Work

MATTHEW GILBERT

CONARI PRESS

First published in 2005 by Conari Press,
an imprint of Red Wheel/Weiser, LLC
York Beach, ME
With offices at:
368 Congress Street
Boston, MA 02210
www.redwheelweiser.com

Library of Congress Cataloging-in-Publication Data
Gilbert, Matthew.
    The workplace revolution : restoring trust in business and bringing meaning to our work / Matthew Gilbert.
      p. cm.
    Includes bibliographical references.
    ISBN 1-57324-921-1
      1. Organizational change. 2. Work-Psychological aspects.
      3. Corporate culture. I. Title.
    HD58.8.G537 2005
    650.1—dc22   2004025970

Typeset in Adobe Garamond, EideticNeo, and Gill Sans by Suzanne Albertson
Printed in Canada
TCP

12 11 10 09 08 07 06 05
 8 7 6 5 4 3 2 1

contents

introduction

For growing numbers of people, the workplace is no longer working. From too many hours and too few benefits to job insecurity and deceitful employers, the affronts to our basic humanity keep mounting. Even if a company meets standard minimums of employer ethics, it's getting more and more difficult to find in our jobs the sustenance and encouragement we need to go on. For most of us, work is a road, not a destination, and it's badly in need of repair. But we don't really expect anyone to fix it; there doesn't seem much that one person can do, and so we keep trudging forward—"I owe, I owe, it's off to work I go"—uncomfortably sandwiched between compromise and despair.

Most of the time we simply shrug our slumping shoulders, thankful to be working at all and dismissing our discontent with a wave of the hand: "Ah, what can I do? It's business!" And yet many of us are waking up to the fact that our deepest selves will no longer settle for the patterns of the past, on the job or off. As we become more sensitized to those needs—which I believe reflect an innate quest for "wholeness," for an expression of self that feeds both heart and mind—it gets harder and harder to ignore them inside the artificial boundaries of our work lives. This "waking up" process cannot simply be shut off. If it encounters an obstacle, such as eight or ten or twelve hours a day of banging one's head against a desk, it will start pushing against it, creating a friction, making noise. When we spend half of our day as if a major part of us didn't exist, a conflict between our heart and our pocketbook forms in which our work life and the rest of our life become increasingly incompatible. Under such conditions we can never feel totally whole or at peace. It is a struggle I have felt deeply, and which inspired me to write this book.

Some years back, I began reading about the possibility of finding one's "true work," the thing you were meant to do on this planet. The idea, as improbable as it sounded, was very appealing. I'd worked at a variety of jobs, most of which I enjoyed to a degree, but there was always an underlying restlessness. I kept feeling that something was missing, some undefined quality that would fill in the gaps and make my work experience an ultimately satisfying one. So I enrolled in a year-long intensive called The Lifework School. I knew that others had "graduated" from this program and were doing—or at least attempting to do—work unique to who they were, created from inside themselves based on a vision or a dream or a secret passion they'd always kept hidden away. I was confident that this new program was just the thing I needed to crack the code of my discontent.

The training was surprisingly rigorous. The program leaders, both psychotherapists, operated from the assumption that a "life work" could only emerge when one's physical, emotional, psychological, and spiritual bodies were healthy and aligned. For one long and challenging year I faced demons I had never known and discovered hope I didn't think I had. When I finally completed the training, I was a different person than when I had started. Somehow a shell had cracked open and a more sensitive, alert, and passionate me emerged.

Still, despite feeling blessed about what I had done and learned, I reluctantly admitted that no one thing had seized me by the lapels and said "Matthew, this is it! Your real mission has begun!" Disappointment was inevitable, but while an ultimate "career path" didn't reveal itself, I did notice that something inside me had been stirred, some ambiguous sense of what felt right to do. It didn't yet have a particular shape, but it was enough to keep me hopeful and moving forward.

Looking back on that time and all that has passed since then, I now realize that in an unexpected way I *had* discovered a deeper purpose for the work I did, but it had more to do with an inner experience than any particular calling or vocation—knowing, for example, that my work was making a positive difference in the world or that my employer respected me or that I didn't have to play games on the job to get things done. It was also about trusting my feelings enough to tell me if I was on the right track. I'm not saying that the job itself or the money I made had no influence on how satisfied I felt about my working life. They did, absolutely. But whenever I prioritized solely for them and not for sources of more intrinsic satisfactions, I ended up in situations that nourished only a part of me, and it was never enough.

At the same time, workplace culture is a dominant and immediate force. Though we usually arrive at our jobs with one set of values, we are abruptly handed another. Business, by definition, is about making money, a process that favors certain qualities over others. Think hierarchy, politics, efficiency, ambition, and greed. As Sarah Ruth van Gelder lamented in *Yes! A Journal of Positive Futures*, "There may be no other place [than work] where the contradiction between our values and aspirations are more apparent. . . . [Our] experience of work is profoundly at odds with what work at its best is about."

One of the reasons I've had such trouble finding solace in the workaday world is that I have always sensed the absence of that first set of values—compassion, patience, trust, integrity, to name a few. I couldn't put a finger on "why" at the time, but whenever I attended various out-of-town functions that were part of a particular job, I'd often gravitate to the edges, watching with wonder and horror as people who didn't know each other made instant best friends in pursuit of the elusive deal. I'd inevitably have a drink too many, forget why I was there, and then slip back to my hotel room and flick on the tube. There were alien encounters out there, and I wasn't about to have any of it. I felt like the proverbial square peg in a round hole, my dark blue jacket and tasteful tie notwithstanding.

I couldn't keep hiding forever, though. I couldn't let "the business of work" keep winning the battle against some vaguely defined humanity that I was clinging to with such tenacity. So I decided to study the workplace in more detail, the cultures and personalities that thrive or die there. Three years ago I wrote *Communication Miracles at Work*, about the importance of authenticity in relationships at work, how easy it is to lose it, and how to get it back. This current book is more ambitious because I'm trying to understand the whole of it—why it's so difficult to be ourselves at work and to find companies that are actually doing more good than harm in the world and to our own spirit. Most of us *endure* our work, the companies we work for, and the people we work with. In recent years, there has been an exodus of nine-to-fivers in pursuit of work that more closely fits their passions and ideals. Sometimes it's by choice as the system finally grinds them down, but more and more frequently it's by necessity as employees fall victim to the pressures of competition and the pursuit of the god called profit. Whatever way you get there, marching to your own drummer is a difficult art to master; it takes luck, patience, hard work, and large doses of self-confidence.

Work for most people evolves (or deteriorates) in more traditional business settings. How can that time be made more satisfying, even in the face of Dilbert-esque neuroses and the demands of a 24/7 world? How has obsession with monetary gain distorted the corporate world and all it touches? How do good intentions go astray? What can be done to revitalize our work lives with a sense of purpose that transcends ego, game playing, and a paycheck?

A few years back, a major research study found that most workers in the West are motivated primarily by one of three things: money (self-explanatory), career development (advancement, accomplishment, expertise), or a "calling" (meaningful work that contributes to a greater good). Of particular interest was the fact that these three categories were not occupation sensitive; in other words, jobs that would seem to have a more natural element of meaningfulness to them (e.g., nursing) had the same motivational distribution among the three groupings as any other. Howard C. Cutler, commenting on this same study in *The Art of Happiness at Work*, noted that the consistency of these groupings across professions "seems to be based more on the psychology of the person and their view of their work, rather than the nature of the work itself." This leads me to believe that the ultimate answer to the question "How can work become more meaningful?" lies within us.

How This Book Is Organized

This book is divided into five sections, each with two to four chapters. The first part—The Hope—begins by acknowledging that while "meaningful work" is an elusive experience in a world where trust in business is at historic lows, the deep need to bring a greater vision to work has seized the spirit of increasing numbers of people and companies. The result: "conscious business," defined in chapter 1 as companies where trust, truth, equality, and unity are replacing control, fear, privilege, and fragmentation as legitimate principles and practices. And as individuals revitalize their own approach to work with renewed purpose and passion, workplace transformation accelerates further.

The second part—The Challenge—is the most difficult. It contains a systematic and often sobering analysis of how the forces of history have turned work in America into an experience of conflict and disappointment for many. The problem is much larger than resolving the age-old "labor-management" dance that has been exhaustively choreographed and critiqued. It is, instead, rooted in an economic culture driven by technology and money and the urgencies of a global marketplace, and the psychological dynamics that tie it all together. A relentless work ethic, the tireless pursuit of profit, and the troubled conflict between business values and human values are all part of the problem. We are prisoners of and participants in this paradigm of desire and fear. And because our workplaces shape us just as we shape them, it's important to look at the role of both.

Parts three and four move in a decidedly more upbeat direction, with specific examples and plenty of tools and ideas that both companies and individuals can use to turn the experience of work into a life-enhancing adventure. For them, the role of work and business in a fractured world becomes a profoundly healing one. From the Corporate Responsibility movement to the integrative principles of Buddhism, there are specific and proven methods for reinvigorating the world of work and the mission of those we work for.

The final part steps more fully outside the box of traditional business practice, suggesting that spirituality and new models of positive organizational management are the future of work in America. Specific examples of people and companies pursuing such ideals make a convincing case that heart, soul, and a revolution in consciousness are the next frontiers of business and work.

My greatest hope is that this book speaks both to the "called" who are struggling to stay true to their original vision, and to those who may be working for other reasons but who are finding that the rewards they sought are not as satisfying as they had hoped and are searching for something more. The system itself will not transform overnight and perhaps not in our lifetimes, but there is still much that we as conscious individuals and managers and executives can do to revitalize our experience of work and change the way that business is done. In the same way that insects can quietly eat away at the foundation of an old home until it weakens and finally gives in, so, too, can each of us, in our own small ways, slowly unscrew the bolts of our aging economic paradigm and our entrapment in it with the small decisions we make every day.

This hope recalls the saying, *"When a man takes one step toward God, God takes more steps toward that man than there are sands in the worlds of time."* The "god" in this case is a vision and a practice of business that has successfully integrated an ultimately human and humane purpose not just into its operations but also into its very reason for being. Work not just to make money but as a way to implement our highest ideals for living consciously, communally, and globally. Naïve? Perhaps. Worth pursuing? Without question.

the hope

CHAPTER 1

A Blueprint for Corporate Change

The opportunities and challenges of the last 20 years in business have been driven by the application of information technology; the next 20 years will be driven by the application of consciousness.

—MICHAEL RENNIE, Principal, McKinsey and Company

When we say that work is meaningless, it generally means different things to different people. For some, boredom has set in or they feel that what they do has no obvious purpose other than a paycheck. For others, it happens when the balance of money made and hours worked goes askew. In some cases defeat sets in when we discover that our employers see us not as human beings but as human resources, movable and expendable pieces on an economic game board. The solutions, then, will vary depending on the circumstance and the person. It can mean changing positions or changing companies or striking out on one's own. Certainly much has been written about such strategies, and they often work—at least for a while. Inevitably, though, for many of us, the discontent will return, perhaps for slightly different reasons but dogging us nevertheless.

It doesn't help that our trust in the intentions of private enterprise remains depressingly low. The stock market's meteoric rise and fall, the spectacular meltdowns of giant companies whose executives made out like bandits, and new economic realities that have more and more people chasing fewer and fewer jobs as work goes overseas or simply disappears, have helped sustain a history of suspicion that business self-interest is dangerously narrow. A 2001 Yankelovich Monitor survey found that more than two-thirds of sampled Americans believed that companies had little interest in whether their actions were serving the public good. According to a *Business Week* study the previous year, 72 percent of Americans believed "business has too much power over too many aspects of American life," while two-thirds felt that "large profits are more important to big companies than developing safe, reliable, quality products for consumers." An October 2002 Harris Poll found that more than half of all adults surveyed felt that Wall Street was so focused on making money that it would break laws to do so if it thought it could get away with it.

Some companies don't even try to disguise their motives. In the beleaguered airlines industry, for example, Delta renegotiated a new contract with its rank-and-file employees that included pay cuts and pension limits while guaranteeing executive pensions in the event of a bankruptcy. Employees at American Airlines also agreed to pay cuts, then threatened to rescind their decision when they learned that the company was about to grant big bonuses to its executive management team while creating a bankruptcy-triggered trust fund for them. The company ultimately backed down on the bonuses, kept the fund, and lost whatever goodwill it could have gained from more principled business dealings. It has since made efforts to repair some of the damage, but as these and numerous other examples indicate, the average employee is getting the short end of several sticks.

Against this background of distrust and disingenuousness, I found a rather startling statistic: In a September 2002 "job satisfaction poll" jointly sponsored by SHRM (the Society of Human Resource Management) and *USA Today*, only 29 percent of a self-selected sample of visitors to *USA Today*'s Web site considered "Meaningfulness of job" as very important to workplace happiness. Only 23 percent said the same of their relationships with coworkers. Both of these percentages were at the bottom of a long list topped by job security, benefits, and "flexibility to balance life and work issues," all legitimate concerns. Human resource professionals polled in the same study had roughly the same response when asked what they thought was most important to an employee's on-the-job experience; only 18 percent chose meaningful work. How sadly right they were.

What are we to make of this? Have necessity and reality turned us into a nation of workplace mercenaries—it doesn't matter the job, so long as we're paid? Do we end up "going for the money" because we don't think we can get any other kind of satisfaction? Have honor and dignity disappeared completely from the work that we do? Would it be a big surprise if they had?

In the 1972 classic *The Homeless Mind: Modernization and Consciousness*, Peter Berger tackled the impact of bureaucracy, technology, and economics on individual consciousness, addressing the issues of honor and dignity in a chapter entitled "The Obsolescence of the Concept of Honor." In it he wrote:

> The concept of honor implies that identity is essentially, or at least importantly, linked to institutional roles. The modern concept of dignity, by contrast, implies that identity is essentially independent of institutional roles.
>
> In a world of honor, the individual discovers his true identity in his roles, and to turn away from the roles is to turn away from himself. . . . In a world of dignity, the individual can only discover his true identity by emancipating himself from his socially imposed roles—the latter are only masks.

Reading these words deepened my understanding of why we have such conflicted feelings about work. If the companies we work for show little evidence of truly humane management or social/environmental/cultural/global conscience, then what incentive do we have to identify positively with them? What would it say about us to buy into their narrow worldview? Perhaps this is why there is such cynicism in the workplace. The implied—and partially articulated—consensus is that we all have to play this dysfunctional game to survive, and by acknowledging the ironies and shared miseries, we stay sane while pretending that we don't really care. In fact it may be the "emancipating" force of our own dignity that brings us to such a cynical brink. It's where we save face.

At the same time, a significant undercurrent of desire exists that work needs to be more than it is. A 2002 study by two consulting firms, Towers Perrin and Gang & Gang called "Working Today: Exploring Employee's Emotional Connection to Their Jobs," found that while senior executives accurately predicted the negative emotional mood of their workforce, they failed to diagnose the right reasons. They overestimated the influence of salary, benefits, job security, and management relations, and underestimated the importance of workload, self-confidence, professional development, recognition, and "feeling connected" to one's work.

Perhaps the way to reconcile the seemingly contradictory findings of the studies mentioned above—one group seeking more "connection" with their work and another who couldn't care less—is that either we are finally waking up to the fact that our jobs offer little to meet our deeper needs for community, self-expression, and service, or we have simply abandoned the idea altogether that work can be much more than a paycheck, thankful, in fact, that it's at least that. Have we been conditioned by society and the dominant corporate paradigm to expect so little from our labors? What will it take for more of us to become proud of where we work and find meaning in what we do?

The Emergence of "Conscious" Business

Despite all the evidence that workplace troubles are as widespread as they've ever been, the terms "conscious business" and "conscious organization" are showing up more often in the lexicon of business speak. They imply an awakening of awareness, a broadening of perspective, a dynamic sense of evolving. They provide a framework for companies and executives to see themselves and their potential from a different point of view.

For a growing number of us, it is no longer enough to exercise our natural skills in the capacity of our jobs. We want to work for companies we believe in, that treat us like human beings, where the bottom line is more than just the next quarter's sales target. In imagining an ideal employer, one that *I* would want to work for, two wishes come to mind:

1. It serves a "triple" bottom line—social, environmental, and financial—and assigns equal priority to each. Such a commitment can infuse each job and each position in that company with meaning and purpose beyond the typical punch in/punch out routine. This can have a powerfully motivating influence on those who work there.

2. It serves the emotional, psychological, and even spiritual needs of its employees. I'm not suggesting that we should expect our employers to be our therapist or surrogate family, but that they actively create workplace environments where we feel safe to be ourselves, inspired to bring more of who we are to what we do. Of course, companies can't make their employees act in such a manner, no matter how benevolent their efforts; that responsibility ultimately is ours. But it's a whole lot easier to answer that call when a company has systems and policies in place that reflect authentic commitment to employee dignity and well-being.

Leadership consultant Richard Barrett has been working with such ideas for years and came up with an evolutionary model of corporate consciousness based loosely on Abraham Maslow's hierarchy of human needs, which he describes in his book *Liberating the Corporate Soul*. Following is how he described them to me:

Level One—Survival Consciousness

This level focuses on financial matters and organizational growth. It includes such values as maximizing profit and shareholder wealth and ensuring employee health and safety. Potentially limiting aspects of this level are generated from fears about survival, leading to such behaviors as excessive control, short-term focus, and exploitation.

Level Two—Relationship Consciousness

Level Two emphasizes the quality of interpersonal relationships between employees and customers/suppliers. It includes values such as open communication, conflict resolution, customer satisfaction, and mutual respect. At the same time, manipulation, blame, and internal competition are more characteristic of companies operating at this level. Entrepreneurship can be low.

Level Three—Self-Esteem Consciousness

Companies at this level are focused on improving work methods and the delivery of services and products using "best practice" systems and processes. "Corporate fitness" is an apt mantra for such businesses. Championed values include productivity, efficiency, excellence, professional growth, and skills development. The potentially limiting aspects of this level result from systems problems and control issues, leading potentially to long hours, arrogance, excessive bureaucracy, and complacency.

Level Four—Transformation Consciousness

This is the "tipping point" for companies motivated by a renewed vision and mission, when control, fear, privilege, and fragmentation give way to trust, truth, equality, and unity. Level Four focuses on continuous renewal and the development of new products and services. It emphasizes such values as accountability, employee participation, teamwork, personal development, and information sharing to overcome the potentially limiting aspects of Levels One to Three.

Level Five—Organization Consciousness ("Internal Cohesion")
The emphasis has now shifted to "corporate well being" and creating an internal sense of community spirit where employees can grow and creativity can flourish. Establishing trust, diversity, integrity, honesty, shared values, cooperation, commitment, fairness, and mutual accountability become the measures of success.

Level Six—Community Consciousness ("Making a Difference")
At this level the emphasis has shifted once again, this time to include a more outwardly oriented perspective that includes deepening and strengthening relationships with customers, suppliers, and a company's local community. Values such as customer collaboration, partnering, strategic alliances, and community involvement are supported, while commitments are made to voluntary environmental and social audits and ensuring long-term sustainability. Internally, Level Six companies focus on employee fulfillment, leadership development, mentoring, and coaching.

Level Seven—Global/Society Consciousness ("Service")
The company has "self-actualized" by committing to help resolve social, human rights, and environmental issues beyond its local community. The focus shifts more deeply to vision and ethics, forgiveness and compassion, and a search for truth and wisdom.

In this model, the first three states reflect different levels of *self-*interest; most of the energy is focused inward. The fourth is the critical point at which a company realizes the limitations of the old operational structure and opens itself to a new one, applying fresh approaches to management and operations. The final three levels represent stages of service to the *common* good, which still includes the well-being of the company but now attended to in a different way than in earlier stages. Barrett makes it clear that no one area—neither "service" nor "survival"—should be emphasized over another for a company to be truly healthy. As a company evolves, there will still be a need for efficiency and control, for example, only (in this model) not at the expense of other more humane and outward-reaching goals. At what level would you place the company *you* work for?

Barrett's model is similar to Spiral Dynamics, a theory of human development based on the work of Dr. Clare Graves and further developed by Dr. Don Beck. Spiral Dynamics organizes humanity and individuals along an eight-stage continuum of psychological and spiritual evolution, from instinctual/survival to what it calls "integrative." Each stage is based on beliefs and values that are often unconscious. People can and do draw from different levels when dealing with the challenges of daily life—for example, doing what we're told at work while also advocating more thoughtful policies—but one psycho/emotional tendency is usually dominant. The current thinking among those who have studied this theory is that humanity as a whole is poised on the edge of a major shift in collective consciousness.

The thing that I find most interesting about these two models is that they suggest that companies evolve and respond to changes in their environment in ways that are similar to what individual people do, each wrestling with the influence and momentum of aging mind-sets while inexorably drawn to more "advanced" states of being. Their destinies, in fact, are intertwined, for when it comes to corporate transformation and meaningful work, organizational and personal change are inseparable.

Still, models are models and theories are theories (and, as we will see later in the book, corporations are not really people). "Conscious business" doesn't happen on a blackboard; it's created intentionally, over time, with high-level commitment and broad participation that can only happen when companies get real with their employees about what's at stake and what they are willing to do, and when each of us responds with equal authenticity. It is not a modest challenge.

The poet David Whyte, who has spoken eloquently on the subject of work and personal transformation, writes in *Crossing the Unknown Sea*:

> It is difficult to be creative and enthusiastic about anything for which we do not feel affection. If the aims of the company are entirely fiscal, then they will engage those whose affections are toward the almighty dollar. If they have a range of qualities or a sense of creative engagement . . . they may get in return something more worthwhile from their people. . . . [Companies] must find a real way of asking people to bring these hidden, heartfelt qualities into the workplace. A way that doesn't make them feel manipulated or the subject of some five-year plan. They must ask for a real conversation.

Moving Beyond Self-Interest

The conversation that Whyte is talking about is bubbling up from the bottom of the organizational chart as human beings continue to evolve faster than the organizations that employ them. For companies to catch up, they must address a wider range of issues than the strictly monetary and play a more active role in shaping a healthier workplace and a more sustainable future for their workforce. Even an "insider" like Michael Rennie, a partner in the Australian office of the blue-chip management consultancy McKinsey & Co., evoked this new vision of work in remarks he recently made to an audience at a "global scenarios" workshop. "[I]n our organization," he proclaimed, "we are finding for the first time ever . . . that to keep people, they have to feel that they are growing personally faster than they could anywhere else." Richard Barrett, in his book *Liberating the Corporate Soul*, writes:

> Who you are is becoming just as important as what you sell. The values that corporations stand for are increasingly affecting their ability to hire the best people and sell their products. . . . Successful business leaders of the 21st century will need to find a dynamic balance between the interests of the corporation, the interest of the workers, and the interests of society as a whole. To achieve this goal they will need to take account of the shift in values taking place in society, and the growing demand for people to find meaning and purpose in their work.

It's a tall order, for the system is us and we are it. And while it has provided many benefits, much has been given up in return. Yet this isn't about overthrowing the system or even advocating some other ism to take its place, but of overhauling it from within, using levers of change that are already present.

This overhaul has nothing to do—at least directly—with helping companies make more money or be more efficient, as most such efforts still tend to focus on. Look no further than the business bestseller shelves to know what I mean. The shift I'm championing is more ideological, more of a change in perspective. It asks each of us to reevaluate the goals that motivate our choices and what we think we need to be happy. It asks companies to develop a genuine concern for the welfare of all as a basis for doing business, and to integrate such values as economic fairness, ecological stewardship, social sensitivity, and human dignity into their operating principles.

All of this requires that we redefine and expand traditional notions of self-interest to include more than just a "what's in it for me or my company" mentality. It's about moving beyond selfishness toward "enlightened" self-interest, which embraces the idea that we are all in this together, that relationships and ethics matter, that no outcome is acceptable that doesn't take into consideration the needs of the whole, and that *how* we do business is of vital importance—the means *are* the ends.

These ideas are similar to the economic principles espoused by Buddhism, which essentially state that the acts of producing and consuming and even acquiring wealth—natural activities of a human life—should nevertheless prioritize for the well-being of not just the individual but of society and the planet as well. They flow from a basic belief in the essential unity and interconnectedness of all life—from the stone to the king to the sun. Buddhism also distinguishes between two kinds of desire: *chanda* and *tanha*. In *Buddhist Economics: A Middle Way for the Marketplace*, P. A. Payutto, Thailand's foremost Buddhist scholar, explains that tanha refers to artificial value, "a commodity's capacity to satisfy the desire for pleasure" and immediate gratification. A primary purpose of advertising is to perpetuate such desires. Chanda, by comparison, is "true" value, the ability of a commodity to satisfy well-being or, stated in another way, relieve suffering. The argument made is that acquisition of a faster car or the latest electronic gadget does not relieve the same level of suffering as does feeding the poor or restoring an ecosystem or doing soulful work. It is a distinctly qualitative difference, one that deeply influences the kinds of economic systems developed and economic decisions made.

Can such ideas coexist with the competitive and individualistic spirit that has long characterized capitalist economics? Coexist and even replace, I hope, if real progress is to be made in solving current problems, meeting future needs, and revitalizing the role of work in our lives. This is not a new vision for corporate America but one that has been left largely on the sidelines. It was best articulated by the late futurist Willis Harman in his book, *Creative Work*:

In new paradigm business, people actualize themselves through meaningful, creative work that emphasizes not only economic profit, but also social responsibility and ecological awareness. Working in humane workplaces that encourage the expression of higher values, such as humanitarian service and social justice, people use the vehicle of work to bring about personal and collective transformation in society.

Harman's vision is certainly inspiring, and yet the reality of today is where we must start, a reality that seems impervious to change. Work is a minefield of ego and emotion, need and want, ambition and failure, where our human failings and strengths cross swords over matters large and small. It is, writes Studs Terkel in *Working* about,

> ulcers as well as accidents, about shouting matches as well as fist-fights, about nervous breakdowns as well as kicking the dog around. It is, above all (or beneath all), about daily humiliations. . . . It is about a search, too, for daily meaning as well as daily bread, for recognition as well as cash, for astonishment rather than torpor; in short, for a sort of life rather than a Monday through Friday sort of dying.

Fortunately, there is much that each of us can do to overcome the torpor that Terkel speaks of, and the rest of this book is dedicated largely to such a quest. At work we have a chance to discover more of who we really are, where we forge and are forged. This is an ongoing process, a journey of discovery in which we are both participant and observer. No matter where you are on the corporate food chain—from the mailroom to the executive suite—there will be opportunities to change your perspective and make different decisions than you have made in the past. Some of those decisions will change your experience, some may change the person you are, and some may even change the company itself.

Deep and sustaining workplace change isn't solely an individual responsibility, though; companies and their leaders must step up as well, and that, too, is covered in the pages that follow. Business beyond avaricious clichés? Business as a force for global good? I hope so; otherwise, we have a shaky future ahead of us.

CHAPTER 2

The Hero's Journey at Work

When nothing seems to help, I go and look at a stonecutter hammering away at a rock perhaps a hundred times without as much as a crack showing in it. Yet at the hundred and first blow it will split in two, and I know it was not that blow that did it—but all that had gone before.
—JACOB RIIS, nineteenth-century social activist

Since we can't shut the system down, and few of us can escape it, we must learn to survive and even thrive within it, seeking creative means to satisfy our longings while doing what we can to change the rules. A good place to begin the process of transforming our experience at work is to make the commitment to actually do it, and then give ourselves permission to believe that real change is possible: "I refuse to accept this. My experience can—and will—be different."

Once we make such a pledge, we immediately face the painful reality of our situation bearing down on us from all sides. How can we possibly turn this thing around? From the moment we walk in the door to the minute we leave, we are immersed in the viscosity of the job. Our discontent becomes a badge of honor, giving us membership in a large and growing club. "Your job sucks, too? I'll drink to that." Cynicism is in, hope is for fools.

Avoiding this reaction has been a significant challenge in my own work life. My first response when I have felt trapped or stressed-out from overwork has been to use all of my energy to obsess on the discomfort, on the dead-end misery of it all. In those times I don't consider that there may be other alternatives, other ways of consciously looking at the problem. Instead, I wait with little expectation for the situation to change by itself. "I am continually struck by how we resist our own potential and hold on to our sense of limitation," Let Davidson laments in his book *Wisdom at Work*. I have learned the hard way—don't we all?—that a different reality is but a choice away. I first experienced this while I was working in Reno as a dice and blackjack dealer.

For a while, my life at the club was the most exciting thing I had ever done, every bit as interesting as the movie images made it seem. Over time, though, it started to wear me down: the noise, the smoke, the monotony, the people. I can remember walking through the doors of the casino where I worked and feeling as if I were suddenly swimming against a strong tide, a psychic ocean thick with energy and emotions that felt worlds apart from my own. By the third or fourth year I had become paralyzed with disenchantment, hyperventilating my anxieties to psych myself for my shift.

One day I whined my discontent to a friend of mine who happened to be a spiritual counselor, and she challenged me to change my experience. "Don't blame others for your troubles, Matthew. You're the one choosing to react as you do. Make different choices." My first response was skepticism: "Yeah, yeah, just another 'change your reality' New Age line. Why don't *you* go down there and work for a few years?" I was, unwilling to acknowledge that I had any control over the situation. But I was desperate and out of options. Realizing I had nothing to lose, I decided to give it a try.

It wasn't easy, but I began by consciously calming myself down and walking into the club with a more accepting attitude. I took things less personally and trained myself not to get negative when the throb of people and noise threatened to engulf me. I tried to just "be myself" and found after a surprisingly short time that my experience *was* changing. I wasn't so exhausted at the end of the night, and the hours miraculously went faster. The noise didn't seem as maddening; I was much more tolerant of the people at my table—even the alcohol-challenged—and I rediscovered the word *amusement* (as in pleased, not park). I can't say that I had transformed the flipping of cards into a performance of Zen-like harmony, but I had enough breakthroughs to really start turning things around, so much so that I could actually visualize *never* leaving my job, flipping plastic and calling out numbers until my hair thinned and my teeth fell out. Interestingly, an opportunity to leave the club came up just a month or two later, and I knew I had been released. But the irony is that by then it almost didn't matter.

Each Moment Counts

Thinking about this experience some years later, I wondered just what had happened. What mechanism was triggered when I accepted my circumstances and basically lived in the moment, whatever it presented me? The answer I stumbled across had its roots once more in Buddhism, in an Eastern worldview of how a wise person relates to the world. Again quoting from *Buddhist Economics*, P. A. Payutto describes it this way:

> A society that views the purpose of life as the pursuit of happiness is one that is recklessly pursuing some future dream. Happiness is seen as somewhere else. Along with this view comes dissatisfaction, impatience, contention, an inability to deal with suffering, and a lack of attention to the present moment.
>
> On the other hand, with a view of life that appreciates the reality of suffering, we pay more attention to the present moment so that we can recognize problems when they arise. We cooperate

with others to solve problems, rather than competing with them to win happiness.

In Reno, it was as if I had flipped a switch. I didn't so much appreciate my suffering as look at myself and my situation honestly, without judgment: this is a real job, with real people, that I have chosen to do. It may not be forever, but it's what I am doing *now*, in the present, which in most spiritual disciplines is the only moment that matters. Once I accepted my job for what it was and then decided to change my experience of it—if not the work itself, then how I approached it—I created a space for other parts of myself to step forward. As I became more aware of my own process and the things that hit my red button, I discovered new tools for dealing with them.

Do you recall that whimsical proclamation, "Wherever you go, there you are"? The closest thing to a koan that Western society can offer, it implies that where we are in life is the product of where we came from, but it also coaxes one to have presence of mind, to look not ahead or behind but at exactly where they are standing (for eight hours a day, in my case). By surrendering to "what is," I had an unexpected experience of what it means to be more fully alive, in the midst of what a few weeks earlier I considered hell itself. What a Eureka! When I later read Eckhart Tolle's *The Power of Now*, describing in remarkable detail how it is to live completely in the moment, I could only shake my head and marvel at his experience *and* his ability to stay there.

Where Purpose Meets Noble Cause

The source of my transformation in Reno, the reason my experience in the casino changed, was not just because I decided to live in the moment and surrender my concerns for the future. It was also propelled by the fact that I made job enjoyment my primary purpose, altering both my relationship with it and my expectations for it. All subsequent behaviors and attitudes, no matter the circumstance, were influenced by this decision. This didn't mean that everything naturally fell into place; old patterns (and insufferable bosses) don't dissolve overnight, and I had my setbacks. But I didn't waiver. I refused to let the job get to me, and it didn't, as long as I stayed true to my purpose and alert to what was going on, inside as well as in front of me. This meant overcoming habitual responses and continually reminding myself of the person I was seeking to be.

In fact, for many of us the deeper meaning in our jobs may not be readily found in the actual work we do but in how it fits into the larger purpose we have for ourselves. Most of us do have some semblance of a purpose, though it may not be an especially grand or long-standing one: controlling our anger, saving money for a new car, and so on. Our purposes tend to be short-term or self-oriented. And yet purpose can be a powerfully galvanizing force, marshalling energies we didn't think we had and inspiring behavior we didn't think we were capable of. "Purpose," writes Richard Leider in *The Power of Purpose,*

> is that deepest dimension within us—our central core or essence—where we have a profound sense of who we are, where we came from, and where we're going . . . a discipline to be practiced day in and day out. . . . Purpose serves as the glue that holds the various aspects of our work together. It gives our work greater focus and energy. It serves as an inner guide by which we can judge appropriate responses to events, people, places, and time. Purpose is the passion that shapes our work life.

If our purpose, our passion, is to make money, then the majority of our decisions at and about work will be driven by that objective. If our primary purpose is to serve or to learn, then our experiences will develop around that. What is your purpose? What values and outcomes are important to you? Are you finding those things in your job?

What purpose *does* work have in your life? Making money, gaining prestige, self-development, family provider, keeping up with the Joneses? What purpose would you like it to serve? If your job lacks meaning, then perhaps the problem is that it also lacks purpose, or that you lack purpose for it, or that whatever purpose you originally had for it no longer sustains you, or that the job is too small for the purpose you do have. "Why am I doing this?" is a common question for those of us frustrated by our work. If the work itself doesn't feed us and the companies we work for don't inspire us, where will our satisfaction come from?

This question brings me inevitably back to Eastern philosophies, not because I think they are superior to Western thought but because I intuitively feel that our cherished notions of work and material achievement need some cross-fertilizing influences. Tarthang Tulku, a religious teacher from the Tarthang Monastery in eastern Tibet and author of several books on the Buddhist principle of right livelihood, says in *Mastering Successful Work*:

> Caring about our work, liking it, even loving it, seems strange when we see work only as a way to make a living. But when we see work as the way to deepen and enrich all our experiences, each one of us can find this caring within our hearts, and waken it in those around us, using every aspect of work to learn and grow.

A similar approach is found in Hinduism in what is called the practice of *karma yoga*, or "the path of God through work." Such a path arose out of the acknowledgment that one's work life needn't be separate from one's spiritual life, that God can be found anywhere, at anytime. Practitioners of karma yoga seek to dissolve the ego and material desires from the work they do in the world, replacing them with a selfless intent to manifest a devotional spirit in all their actions. Much is written about work as a form of spiritual expression in the *Bhagavad-Gita*, a sacred Hindu text. Mahatma Gandhi, whose nonviolence campaign against the ruling British in his home country of India changed history, was a devoted disciple of the *Bhagavad-Gita*.

Gandhi started out as a lawyer, moving to South Africa after a string of failures in India. There he experienced discrimination for the first time, but still had to make a living. His very first case involved a disagreement about money between two parties who were blood relatives. He soon realized that the facts were on his client's side, but he also concluded that if the case went to trial, a long court battle would be unavoidable, driving family members further apart. So he took another tack: talking to both sides and convincing them to settle out of court. As Eknath Easwaran writes in his biography of Gandhi:

> Gandhi was ecstatic. "I had learned," [Gandhi] exclaimed, "the true practice of law. I had learnt to find out the better side of human nature and to enter men's hearts. I realized that the true function of a lawyer was to unite parties riven asunder." Without realizing it, Gandhi had found the secret of success. He began to look on every difficulty as an opportunity for service, a challenge which could draw out of him greater resources of intelligence and imagination. In turning his back on personal profit or prestige in his work, he found he had won the trust and even love of white and Indian South Africans alike.

Not everyone is capable of such Gandhi-like wisdom and action—there's certainly no halo over my head—but the story of his awakening brings our own workplace challenges into sharper focus. Perhaps finding satisfaction and meaning in our jobs will depend on whether we discover the "noble cause" in them—for example, how our work serves others—or whether we can successfully bring our own noble cause to it. Psychologist Martin Seligman, in his book *Authentic Happiness*, writes that "feeling positive about knowing you are using your highest strengths and virtues . . . in the service of something you believe is bigger than you" will lead to a happy and meaningful life.

Applying such a larger sense of purpose to our work life can help guide us through difficult decisions and even mold us into wiser and more loving beings. This is not simply a matter of changing attitudes but of overhauling previous motivations, replacing secular intentions with what some might describe as spiritual ones, and small purposes with larger ones.

Such a voyage begins with a belief in its worthiness and a faith in its outcome—your basic hero's journey. There is no single guaranteed path to more meaningful work; each of us will forge our own way through a variety of challenges, everything from insensitive bosses and oppressive work cultures to job insecurity and financial pressures. Achieving workplace "sainthood" is much closer to a marathon than a hundred-yard dash. It would be easier if the companies we worked for made enlightened workplaces their priority, but we can never count on that. And yet when we commit to transforming our experience at work, changes will be felt almost immediately. They may be as small as leaving the house earlier in the morning with better energy, or come as unexpected shifts in perception—insight into a manager's (or our own) anger or clarity about a positive career move. The key is remembering our purpose and mission and attending to our experiences with that awareness. We have more control over our fate than we have led ourselves—and been led—to believe, and it is time to exercise that power.

At the same time, we do confront very real challenges that make it difficult to experience the kind of deep satisfaction at work that many of us seek. Despite growing pressure to reshape business strategies in more humane and socially responsible ways, many companies will fail to do so or progress will be painfully slow. Even when we work for companies that make us proud, there will be times when our best efforts to meet the challenges in front of us will be stymied by forces seen and unseen. No matter who we work for or what we do, there will always be obstacles to bringing more of our self to our work, to finding meaning and purpose in a world that often feels more like a battleground than a place to experience our common humanity and potential.

~~~

The profit-seeking nature of business and capitalist economics—at least as it has come to pass—does play a significant role in what we can realistically expect from our jobs; our employer's primary mission has been limited in scope from the start. Ultimately, though, the challenge for companies to pursue a larger vision of what it means to be in business must also be met by each one of us, whether it's how we treat coworkers or taking a stand against a particular injustice. Just as the companies we work for need to find the "noble cause" in their corporate mission, so too must we as individuals working in that system uncover our own noble intentions toward work. If we truly seek more meaning in our jobs, if we are tired of checking most of our humanity at the office door, then it's time for a workplace perspective that aims for higher ideals despite the harsh realities we face every day.

And yet, acknowledging and sometimes confronting that reality must become part of the solution. Of what purpose is a hero's journey if there aren't a few dragons to slay? From stress and overwork to the influence of corporate culture on the quality of our work environment, there are legitimate challenges to making real progress toward a more satisfying experience at work. Some of these challenges are simply part of the society we live in, while others have become hardwired into corporate missions and workplace cultures. The next few chapters examine the most powerful of these forces.

PART 2

The chaLLenge

CHAPTER 3

Time and Money: The Endless Quest

*If you're not going Mach II with your hair on fire, then there's
something wrong.*
—KATIE BILL, "Are We Working Too Hard?"
(Seattle Times, October 12, 2003)

In a materialistically driven society such as ours, work plays a necessary and dominant role, with the emphasis increasingly on *dominant*. The idea of experiencing more meaning in our work might feel more achievable if we had the time to even consider it. Our dependence on material comforts plus the normal demands of daily living—paying the bills, going to meetings, dealing with family crises—keep us running, running, running, working, working, working. In our society's version of progress, we are what we have and we never have enough, a belief that our economic culture cultivates and depends on.

As reported by Juliet Schor in *The Overspent American*, a 1986 Roper poll asked a sample of Americans how much annual income they would need to fulfill all their dreams. Their answer: $50,000. Eight years later that figure had climbed to over $100,000. One can only guess what the number is today as financial planners earnestly warn us that a million dollars in the bank may not be enough to finance our retirement! The most telling—and perhaps most disturbing—of the research findings quoted by Schor charting this "culture of materialism" are the results of a thirty-year study on the aspirations of college freshman, nine million of whom were queried on fifteen hundred campuses. When asked in 1968 to identify the most important reasons they decided to go to college, 83 percent chose "Develop a meaningful philosophy of life" while 43 percent chose "Be very well off financially." By 1996 those figures had essentially reversed, creating enormous pressures either to get ahead or to keep from falling behind. It should be no surprise that antidepressants remain the best-selling category of prescription drugs in America, with annual sales of well over $10 billion and annual increases in the double digits.

This massive shift in priorities has created on-the-job problems as well. A slew of new surveys about work seem to confirm that on-the-job stress, not to mention the personal costs associated with it, is on the rise. For example:

- Of 750 employees and 200 employers nationwide surveyed in 2002 by Cigna Behavioral Health, 44 percent said their jobs were more stressful than they were a year ago. When asked what they were worried about, 51 percent mentioned the economy, 40 percent said they were "troubled by the heightened distrust in corporate America," and 40 percent cited fear of job loss.
- In a nationwide survey of 1,805 adults eighteen years and older carried out in 2002 by the Tylenol corporation, 62 percent named "lack of time" as a major source of stress, and too many hours at work as the most significant reason for it. Fifty-eight percent said that financial concerns were causing significant tension, including not being able to save money or pay bills on time, the high cost of living, and not being able to afford the things they wanted.
- Another nationwide survey taken in 2002 called "Coping with the Changing Realities of Work and Life," sponsored by GLS Consulting, Inc., queried 561 women and 165 men in "new

economy" companies. Among the more pertinent findings: 41 percent said that workplace stress had worsened, and 56 percent reported not having the emotional strength and energy left for life outside of work. The study also concluded, "Women no longer report a simultaneous sense of 'exhilaration and exhaustion' as they did in [the company's 2000 study]. While the exhaustion remains, the exhilaration is absent."

- The problems aren't limited to the United States. In Britain, for example, a 2002 survey carried out by *Management Today* and the Department of Trade and Industry's (DTI) Work-Life Balance Campaign found that the number of workers putting more than sixty hours a week into their jobs had increased 33 percent in just the last two years. The number of women working similar hours more than doubled. In another U.K. survey, 64 percent of 500 people interviewed said they had experienced stress at work over the last twelve months, up 11 percent from a year ago.

The notion of work as a calling, a vocation, a place to express some of humankind's more noble virtues, has clearly fallen on hard times. The same motivations that drove our ancestors to levels of industriousness never before seen in this country have given us almost everything we've ever wanted except peace of mind. The result: More and more people are simply wearing out. When Benjamin Franklin immortalized the maxim, "Time is money," he had no idea what he had helped to unleash. Commenting in the *Financial Times* on the importance of "cocooning" in American life, Syracuse University professor Robert Thompson noted, "We are in a period in our culture where we're looking in our leisure time for things that will anesthetize us." And if there is a trend here, it's going in the wrong direction.

"We're logging more hours on the job than we have since the 1920s," says Joe Robinson, author of *Work to Live: The Guide to Getting a Life.* "Almost 40 percent of us work more than 50 hours a week."

The Bureau of Labor Statistics has reported that the typical American worker already puts in 350 more hours a year—an almost nine-week difference—than his or her European counterpart. Not surprisingly, we are among the most productive workers in the world. But what good is such industriousness if we can't step back to enjoy its fruits? The bureau also found that Americans have the shortest vacation allotment of any country in the industrialized world: 8.1 days after a year on the job and a whopping 10.2 days after three years, *at our employer's discretion.* Compare this to the legally mandated month of down time that typifies workers in many other countries where lifestyle quality, objectively *or* subjectively measured, is arguably equal to or even higher than our own. To wit: The Federal Reserve Board found that "Europe had a higher productivity growth rate in fourteen of the nineteen years between 1981 and 2000" than the United States. Robinson himself found that U.S. companies implementing a three-week vacation policy reported increases in both profits and productively and decreases in turnover.

Think of the last vacation you took—assuming you even took one. Was it sufficiently relaxing so that you returned to work physically, emotionally, and mentally renewed? Did you make some time for solitude, for checking in with the deeper parts of you that draw from the soul and often reveal necessary wisdom? Or did you need a vacation to recover from a vacation that tried to fit too much into too little?

As if all this wasn't enough, the Department of Labor, at the prodding of business groups and White House officials, recently issued a rewrite of wage and hour regulations "which would turn anyone who holds a 'position of responsibility' into a salaried employee who can be required to work unlimited overtime for no extra pay." In other words, change an employee's title to manager and—voilà!—instant indentured servant. Both the Senate and the House of Representatives voted to block the new regulations, but as of this writing, President

Bush has vowed to override their objections. If he succeeds, millions of middle-income workers would be affected.

The Morality of Materialism

There is nothing inherently wrong with working hard. In fact, many of us are proud to have a chance to put our skills to work; having a job is usually a sign of societal acceptance, that who we are and what we do is valued in some way. 'Tis better to be overworking than not working at all.

But in recent years the workplace has become more foe than friend. The feelings and interactions that make us human are more often shared on the sly or delivered unexpectedly than woven into the fabric of our daily work life. Most of us are trapped in a business paradigm that is still narrowly focused on one thing—making money—and that single-minded purpose bows to a specific set of values that all who work must obey. Making money isn't all bad, of course. The pursuit of wealth has driven innovations that have led to spectacular improvements in our standard of living. Creature comforts have never been so numerous or so accessible. But the price of these achievements is becoming more obvious. From disappearing wildlife and wars over oil to wage inequalities and stress levels off the chart, we are suffering the effects of a work ethic and a business culture that have pushed most noble intentions to the margins.

"Wealthism," writes Marjorie Kelly, the founder of *Business Ethics* magazine and author of *The Divine Right of Capital,* "is not only about believing wealthy persons are superior to others; it's also about believing money is the measure of all things, that our self-worth resides in what we earn and what we own, that working long hours to earn money is more important than spending time with family and friends."

A *Time* magazine cover story, discussing the remarkable financial achievements of the Mormon Church since its founding in the early

1800s, said that its hard-earned success was a reflection of our nation's moral declaration that "material achievement remains the earthly manifestation of virtue." What we call the "Protestant work ethic" has become the defining characteristic of work in the West, the primary means by which one accumulates wealth and exercises a moral certitude. This convenient intersection of materialism and righteousness has turned hard work and getting ahead into a national religion with skyscraper churches and commandments of production and conquest. It's a religion that is devoid of spiritual life.

"Consider today's economic system," wrote Glenn Pascall, an award-winning economics columnist, in a 1998 *Seattle Times* essay. "Its god is performance. Its high priests are financial analysts. Its royalty are large shareholders. Its servants are line managers. Its slaves are numberless Dilberts." And in *Ethics in Business: Faith in Work*, James Childs compares the ideals of Christian business ethics to the realities of today's workplace and concludes that the vast inequities in the current system regarding salaries and status are hardly evidence that "the biblical ideal is at work. . . . [C]ommitment to . . . conspicuous achievement as the key to meaning in life can be a harsh and demanding regimen that could cause us to compromise our own best qualities and some of our most precious values."

The original spirit of the Western work ethic saw work not as a means to a private end but a vehicle of service with a spiritual and devotional cast. Material accumulation devoid of any greater responsibilities was unheard of. It may seem unreasonable in today's 24/7 workplace to expect anyone to put work and devotion in the same sentence, but it certainly makes sense to bring more of our best selves to the work that we do: pushing personal boundaries, discovering true compassion, addressing global concerns. Why shouldn't a work life be filled with such things as these?

The answer is complicated—its pursuit a big reason why I wrote this book—but a good place to start is with a short history of how the

Protestant work ethic, a cliché tossed around like so many losing lottery tickets, evolved from a way to serve God into a mantra of acquisition.

A Short History of Work

In pre-Reformation times, the material world was seen as something evil, something to escape from. Work was "a burden and a tribulation" that followed from original sin, "humankind's turning away from God and his plan."

The Benedictine monks of the sixth century were exceptions to this point of view. These pious men of God considered work, along with prayer and recreation, as the primary means by which one could grow closer to the Almighty. In carrying out the various duties of their station, the inventive monks found ways to standardize their tasks and create greater efficiencies in order to free themselves for more meditation and prayer. When combined with their natural thriftiness, the result was a saving of monies that were then reinvested in better tools, which saved even more time, and thus a pattern was set. They were literally "working for God" from a place of total devotion and surrender. There are some who feel that the Benedictines were the first true capitalists.

It wasn't until the Reformation of the 1500s, however, that the idea of work was finally transformed from a yolk of duty into a vehicle for serving both God and humanity through the financial success of one's efforts. The principal architects of this shift, both better known for confronting what they felt was the "spiritual laziness" of the Catholic Church in Rome, were the German priest Martin Luther and the French theologian John Calvin.

Luther, the man who nailed ninety-five theses to the door of a Saxon church and started the Protestant religious movement, brought a new perspective to the role of work in God's plan by introducing the idea of work as *vocation*, a calling in which one uses all of his skills and intentions to serve God by serving others. As Oliver Williams and John Houck write in *The Judeo-Christian Vision and the Modern Corporation*:

> Luther taught that one's occupation in the world was not to be taken lightly, for doing the task well was the way to serve God and to give thanks for divine justification. This conviction provided motivation for high performance in one's station in life, whether it be as a scholar, craftsperson, or laborer.

Calvin's contribution was to conclude that since everything came from God, work had its place at the Lord's table, especially as it made life better for all. "We know," he said, "that men were created for the express purpose of being employed in labour of various kinds, and that no sacrifice is more pleasing to God than when every man applies diligently to his own calling, and endeavors to live in such a manner as to contribute to the general advantage." For Calvin, one worked for the glory of God; by serving others, one served God.

There were a couple of catches in Calvin's vision, though, the most troublesome of which was his doctrine of *predestination*. It essentially stated that one's destiny at the end of life was already preordained by God and there was little one could do to alter it; you either were chosen or you weren't. This of course led to a great deal of "salvation anxiety" as many people agonized over their fate. How is one to know? Is it a matter of faith, birth, chance? It was left to the newly reformed pastors to step forward and offer some guidance. They said there were *signs* of conscription, evidence that one was among the saved, and one of those signs was material success. "Thus everyone struggled to ensure that businesses were profitable," Williams and Houck write, "and this produced the driven quality in the 'Protestant ethic.' Although the pastors encouraged people to live frugally, to be austere, they were also counseling industriousness and persistence."

Calvin also preached that wealth through work was a scourge if it caused one to value it above holiness and commitment to God. To this the pastors had another answer: the doctrine of *stewardship*, which held that wealth was a trust to be kept *for the common good*. This ultimate confluence of vocation, stewardship, hard work, frugality, and God ushered in what German sociologist Max Weber called the "fundamental element of the spirit of modern capitalism: Rational conduct on the basis of calling." It was Weber who coined the phrase "Protestant work ethic." Importantly, he cautioned in his seminal work *The Protestant Ethic and the Spirit of Capitalism* that one's calling wasn't to be used as a means to ungodly ends but as a way to carry out God's personal mission for you through the work and skills given.

And so the die was cast: Ambition and hard work were blessed as religious virtues, and financial achievement (properly "stewarded," of course) became the primary measure of how well one was following divine direction. Not surprisingly, a veneer of righteousness settled over those who honored God and mastered their fate by pouring themselves into their work. Those who weren't so industrious—no matter the reason—or whose efforts barely kept them a farthing ahead of the tax man, were dismissed as lazy or sinful even as they slid helplessly (or deservedly!) into impoverishment and disease.

From Vocation to Exploitation

Over time, our culture lost sight of the ethic's more conservative and spiritual emphasis—a means to grow closer to God—and veered in a more secular direction. The more cynical among us would probably describe its new identity as the Protestant Wealth Ethic.

"In the centuries following the Protestant reformation," wrote Sharon Beder, author of *Selling the Work Ethic: From Puritan Pulpit to Corporate PR*, "the emphasis on work as a religious calling was gradually superseded by a materialistic quest for social mobility and material success." This was a period of immense technological innovation—the Industrial Revolution of the eighteenth and nineteenth centuries—in which capitalism and tools of mass production replaced the individual skills of the trades as the dominant business model in England and America. It was also a time when the workforce began to split into two camps: the haves and the have-nots. The haves grew wealthier as the value of their "capital" increased with every new investment, while the have-nots struggled with new workplace realities that had little to do with mastering one's fate and a lot to do with simple survival. Craftsmanship was replaced by discipline and anonymity while purpose and fulfillment were left at the factory door.

These patterns continued well into the twentieth century until the Information Age came to the rescue and transformed the workplace once again, opening up significantly more opportunities for individuals to bring more of themselves to their jobs. Instead of physically demanding, mind-numbing repetition, the new jobs asked much more from us. They required thinking and cooperation and discernment. The advent of computer technology unleashed a flood of creativity that was often bottom-up—the folks in the trenches were the ones coming up with the innovations, and they were rewarded for their efforts. New management strategies emphasized empowerment and decentralized decision making. It seemed that the culture of work was on the crest of a new paradigm.

But the Information Age has proved to be more a distraction from than a liberator of positive corporate values and workplace harmony. Such new and evolving technologies as cell phones and the Internet grew quickly beyond hobbies, introducing new levels of organizational management and workplace flexibility but also accelerating the influence of business over our lives. Once a catchy moniker of efficiency, "24/7" has become a sign of economic relentlessness. A recently published novel by Max Barry called *Jennifer Government* imagines a futuristic world where employees take the name of the companies they work for—John Nike, Calvin McDonalds. Given the growing number of hours that many people are working these days, it is not such a far-fetched notion. The demands of commerce have taken their toll, both in perpetuating a culture of materialism and in degrading our very *experience* of work. There is deep cynicism, a lack of trust, a grudging surrender to the powers that be. It really is a jungle out there.

At the same time, the forces of personal ambition and greed unwittingly unleashed by the Protestant work ethic and its distortions over time were never far away, exploding in a crescendo of avarice with the stock market crash of 2000 followed by the spectacular collapse of several major companies. This may have made us more wary, but it didn't slow down our preoccupation with achieving "the good life."

The Prayer of Jabez: Breaking Through to the Blessed Life by Bruce Wilkinson has sold more than six million copies since it came out in 2000 and, like the Chicken Soup phenomenon of the nineties, spawned multiple derivatives. The book asserts that the mere daily repetition of a simple prayer asking for God's blessings will bring to its adherents more than they could possibly hope for in the name of doing God's work. Unfortunately, Wilkinson emphasizes the external rewards, the "enlarging of territory," that God will bestow on those who seek such divine intercession, not on how much more like Christ (who, as I recall, didn't preside over great swaths of land) that person could become by devotional commitment. *Forbes* magazine explained the appeal of the book this way: "Asking God for a life of plenty . . . constitutes a spiritual act."

It is certainly understandable to want to be free of survival worries or compensated justly for our efforts, but where do you draw the line, how much is enough, what is the underlying motivation? The popularity of the book echoes earlier Christian views equating material success with godliness—wealth not simply as a gift from God but a sign of his favor and the purity of one's faith. "When did the accumulation of wealth become the number one career concern?" the pastor at a local church lamented one Sunday. "What happened to just using God's gifts as best as one can?"

Fighting Back

More and more people are starting to resist the momentum of their materialistic and time-stealing treadmill. Typing "simple living movement" in Yahoo!, for example, yielded over one million page references. At the top of the list was The Simple Living Network, based on David Wampler's work with The Institute for Earth Education. Since 1994, TSLN has been helping folks reconsider what quality of life really means while advocating personal solutions to managing and reducing their consumptive ways that take into account culture, personality, and lifestyle. Their Web site (www.simpleliving.net) features study groups, tips for beginners, networking resources, and more than five hundred "simple living" tools and products, including the Your Money or Your Life Web site based on the best-selling book by Vicki Robin and Joe Dominguez.

The most recent response to slowing down the frantic pace of our work and personal lives is the Take Back Your Time movement, "a nationwide initiative to challenge the epidemic of overwork, overscheduling and time famine that now threatens our health, our families and relationships, our communities and our environment." The movement, started in 2003, even has its own day—October 24—chosen because it falls nine weeks before the end of the year, the difference in time between how long Americans work each year and how long their European counterparts work.

In addition to plenty of consciousness-raising activities, this advocacy group (www.timeday.org) offers both personal and institutional suggestions for achieving a healthier work/life balance. "If our economy is not designed to help people create balanced lives and make time for such things as family and community," asks John deGraaf, author of

Take Back Your Time: Fighting Overwork and Time Poverty in America and a principal architect of the initiative, "then what is it for?" He notes that Europeans have generally put their productivity gains into creating more time for themselves, while Americans put their gains into making even more money and buying more stuff. What kind of values are behind such decisions?

Transforming the role of work in our lives is a step-by-step process that must also acknowledge the impact of our lifestyle and our culture. Each of us makes choices every day on how to navigate this world, based on values we've internalized over the years and the demands of living in a techno-capitalist society. The more aware we are of those choices and their influence on the quality of our lives, the better equipped we'll be to make smarter ones. They may not always be easy to make, but knowing there are options such as those mentioned above is an important first step to regaining some control over the outcomes we live with.

At work those choices can feel more limited and elusive given the lopsided nature—both explicit and implied—of the contract between employer and employee. The pressure to "go with the flow" can be overpowering. The next two chapters look more closely at the modern corporation and the typical workplace, how they shape our experience on the job, and what that means in the pursuit of more purposeful work.

CHAPTER 4

The Soulless Company

It will be a hard pill for many Americans to swallow—the idea of doing with less so that big business can have more. . . . Nothing that this nation, or any other nation, has done in modern economic history compares in difficulty with the selling job that must be done to make people accept the new reality.
—*Business Week* (October 12, 1974)

The *Business Week* quote above had a chilling effect on me when I first discovered it. It confirmed my deep frustration, disappointment, and anger at what I feel has gone on in the name of preserving the "American way of life" and maintaining our cherished "standard of living," both of which are endlessly championed by corporate America, their government lobbyists, and reelection-driven politicians. At the same time, I think it's important—and ironic—to acknowledge that the "standard of working" in many of the companies who employ us seems at odds with the spirit of contentment and progress implied by this quest for a better life. The further irony, of course, addressed in the previous chapter, is that our cherished "way of life" often feels like a race that has no finish line.

It's certainly no secret that people get frustrated with the companies they work for and the quality of their work environment; there will always be reasons to grumble about our jobs and our employers. But if meaningful work is what we seek and deeper satisfaction the goal, then we must dig below the surface of our day-to-day discontents and examine the roots of workplace dysfunction. Those roots extend well back in time, revealing how economic and legislative forces have conspired to give business and industry almost limitless power to create an ideal economic world—for themselves.

The Birth of Corporate America

As history has taught us, this country was born in large part from confrontation with excessive corporate power. The Boston Tea Party was a revolt against the monopolistic power of England's East India Company, which was dumping its unsold tea in the American colonies at below-market prices to stave off bankruptcy. Britain's Tea Act of 1773 repealed export taxes on East India's tea, giving them unfavorable advantage over colonial merchants. Although the Tea Act reduced the price of tea for the colonists, they nevertheless saw it as another example of market manipulation and undercutting the livelihood of local businessmen (and a few local smugglers). The colonists were already sending a steady supply of natural resources to their imperial masters in England by way of the Hudson Bay Company; the rigging of the tea market turned out to be one exploitation too many, and over the sides of British ships the crates of tea were tossed (the cost of the ruined tea is estimated to have exceeded one million dollars in today's prices).

Not surprisingly, when the colonies finally broke away and the United States of America was born, corporations played a nominal role in the vision of the new country's future. In fact, they weren't even mentioned in the Constitution. It was left to the states to "charter" their existence, which they did only when necessary to serve "the public good." Those companies legislated into being faced stiff controls on their operations. For example:

- They had a limited shelf life: twenty to fifty years.
- States could revoke a company's charter at any time if they felt that harm to the citizenry was being done.
- Corporations were prevented from making political contributions or in any way influencing legislation.
- State legislatures set the prices that corporations could charge for their products or services.
- Perhaps most remarkably, shareholders were personally liable for any debts that the company could not pay off.

The mood of the day was best represented by moral philosopher and economist Adam Smith, whose book *The Wealth of Nations*—considered by many to have inaugurated modern economics—extolled the virtues of a truly free and competitive market, liberated from the oppressive influence of state *and* corporate power.

These ideals didn't last, though. The societal unrest that followed the Civil War fractured the government and opened the door to a wave of corporate influence and legislative sellouts. As stakeholders grew savvier to the ways of law and legislators and the Supreme Court became filled with former corporate lawyers, restrictions on commercial activities began to erode. A new wave of wealthy industrialists including John D. Rockefeller, Cornelius Vanderbilt, Andrew Carnegie, and James Mellon used their considerable influence and resources to expand and extend the legal protections of corporate power. The fight started draining from formerly vigilant watchdog groups. The "common good," once a declaration of citizen empowerment, was redefined to favor economic ends. As summarized by Barbara Knox, Ph.D., in an article titled "The Trouble with Corporations,"

> . . . appointed judges gave privilege after privilege to corporations: the right to take private property with minimal compensation; elimination of jury trials to determine corporation-caused harm. . . . Courts ruled that workers were responsible for causing their

own injuries on the job. . . . Wages, hours and rate laws of the states were tossed out. Courts construed the common good to mean maximum production, no matter who was hurt or what was destroyed. Corporate competition without citizen interference was enshrined.

The final blow to those who felt that corporate power was expanding at a dangerous rate came in 1886 when Supreme Court Justice Morrison Remick Waite stated in *Santa Clara County v. Southern Pacific Railroad* that "The court does not wish to hear argument on the question whether the provision in the Fourteenth Amendment to the Constitution, which forbids a State to deny to any person within its jurisdiction the equal protection of the laws, applies to these corporations. We are all of opinion that it does." In the Court record of the case, the court reporter wrote: "The defendant Corporations are persons within the intent of the clause in section 1 of the Fourteenth Amendment to the Constitution of the United States, which forbids a State to deny to any person within its jurisdiction the equal protection of the laws."

Remarkably, no one questioned the reporter's interpretation of the judge's comment, and a new era of corporate power and influence was inadvertently launched. Corporations were now officially recognized as "natural persons" with all the protections of the Bill of Rights.

"Recognized as persons," explains William Meyers of the Redwood Coast Alliance for Democracy, "corporations lose much of their status as subjects of the government. Although artificial creations of their owners and the governments, as legal persons they have a degree of immunity from government supervision. Endowed with the court-recognized right to influence both elections and the law-making process, corporations now dominate not just the U. S. economy, but the government itself."

Corporate Personhood Revealed

If corporations are treated as "people," and these people are taking over our world, what kind of people are they? This is just the question asked by author and legal scholar Joel Bakan in his book *The Corporation: The Pathological Pursuit of Profit and Power* and in his same-titled Canadian documentary (which won a major award at the Sundance Film Festival and is now the highest-grossing documentary in Canadian history).

The book examines the history of corporate power and describes how Bakan, working with an FBI profiler and a standard checklist of personality traits from *The Diagnostic and Statistical Manual of Mental Disorders*, found a nearly item-by-item match—amoral, deceitful, manipulative, self-interested—between corporate behavior and the personality disorder known as "psychopathic," primarily characterized as devoid of social or moral conscience that will do anything in the pursuit of personal gratification. In this case that gratification is called profit.

The film is particularly revealing as Bakan brings together both critics of the system—Michael Moore, Noam Chomsky, and Richard Grossman, to name a few—and advocates, including Milton Friedman and Peter Drucker ("If you find an executive who wants to take on social responsibilities, fire him. Fast."). One of the more dispassionate assessments is provided by investment manager Robert Monks, who describes the corporation as "an externalizing machine, in the same way that a shark is a killing machine. There isn't any question of malevolence or of will. The enterprise has within it, and the shark has within it, those characteristics that enable it to do that for which it was designed."

True enough. But while the design itself can be objectively deconstructed, economist David Korten believes that it masks a far more sinister intention. He writes in *The Post-Corporate World*,

Because the corporation is populated by the people who work in its employ, there is a tendency to think of the institution almost as a living person, an illusion cultivated by corporate relations and given legal standing by court rulings. Yet the corporation is not a person and it does not live. It is a lifeless bundle of legally protected financial rights and relationships brilliantly designed to serve money and its imperatives. It is money that flows in its veins, not blood. The corporation has neither soul nor conscience.

And while the phenomenon of corporatism really has taken on a life of its own, let's not forget that the architects of this beast aren't robots or computer programs but flesh-and-blood human beings making decisions every day about the kind of world they think we should live in.

The Unholy Marriage of Power and Profit

A variety of constitutional amendments, especially the First (free speech) and Fourteenth (citizenship, due process), have been invoked over the years to protect and consolidate corporate power and extend corporate influence. On a practical level, this means that companies can keep safety inspectors from randomly entering their buildings, hire lobbyists and contribute to political campaigns, and bend truth-in-advertising laws, benefiting from the same rights extended to human beings without the liabilities or moral conscience. They can, in short, do almost whatever they want to further an agenda—maximizing profit—that Congress and the courts codified in the early 1900s in a series of decisions making corporations legally accountable to their financial investors. Shareholder demands for short-term gain thus heavily influence the choices of corporate executives.

A neighbor of mine has worked for the phone company for almost thirty years. Back when he started, he recalls, it was truly a local business with no more than a dozen employees. But over time it kept getting bought by larger companies. After each merger, he says,

> more hierarchy, more bureaucracy, and more centralization were added. Soon each of us had a number. Employee evaluations were sent to corporate and sometimes marked down (e.g., from a 5—the highest—to a 4)! Those people didn't even know us, but those markdowns made it more difficult to justify a raise. We started to lose service people. The customer call center was moved to a "right to work" [no unions] state. Our service levels started to drop. When I asked my supervisor what could be done, he told me "Forget customer service. It's all about share price."

"Ticker shock" is thus to be avoided, even if it means selling banned pesticides to desperate farmers in Third World countries, depleting the national seed stock to assert monopoly control over the future of our food, or simply cutting corners and giving customers less than what they pay for. And if the quarterly reports start to lose their luster, corporate bean counters enlist a variety of dubious techniques to massage the numbers in the right direction. This was especially evident during the Internet and technology bubble of the late nineties and early 2000s, when the stock market became a kind of Wall Street casino that seduced willing investors out of billions and perhaps trillions of dollars that simply evaporated into thin air (and into executive bank accounts). The U.S. economy and those who depend on it are still paying for that loss, money that could have been used in countless other more thoughtful and constructive ways.

Corporate power has not gone completely unchecked, of course. The creation of the Better Business Bureau and the Underwriters Laboratory in the late nineteenth century, for example, built modest levels of trust into business transactions, while the advent of unionism to combat low wages and unhealthy working conditions took some of the steam from the wealth-producing engines of the early twentieth century. The rebellious 1960s "questioned authority" and challenged a system that was cleaving the population more and more into the wealthy and everyone else. Consumer activists such as Ralph Nader forced companies to take responsibility for their most egregious actions, while today's many activist groups work tirelessly for economic justice and accountability. Sarbanes-Oxley, a bill passed on July 30, 2002, in the wake of a tsunami of corporate scandals, finally put some teeth into provisions for ethics and financial reporting, despite rigorous efforts by the White House and corporate lobbyists to weaken it.

But these eruptions of discontent and rehabilitation have only slowed the ascendance of corporate clout. In the early hours of a new millennium, the institution of business has never been more influential.

With a willfulness and single-mindedness that borders on obsession, Corporate America has achieved for itself carte blanche to do what it wants in the name of making money, systemically diminishing the public good in favor of private gain. Through mergers, downsizing, sophisticated PR, control of government policies through special interest money, and even influence over "experts" in the scientific community, industry leaders have consolidated their power and put themselves in a position to call most of the shots. The result has been unprecedented wealth and influence in the hands of a few with little accountability, and no industry is immune.

Traditional yardsticks of economic health such as GDP (Gross Domestic Product) growth remain sacred, no matter how that growth occurs. Car wrecks and lawsuits and lung cancer and wetlands destruction make positive contributions. When they aren't pushing employees to perform, companies are pushing their "target markets" to buy, with advertising campaigns that reach deeper and deeper into the fabric of society. "Co-branding" ventures stamp corporate logos on everything from toys and movie characters to video games and theme parks. Those same logos, along with donations and even curriculum materials, are showing up in schools across the country ("revenue enhancements," most administrators will tell you). In short, it has become abundantly clear that the capitalist imperative has gone well beyond any pretense of performing "good works" or "serving the public good." It is simply serving itself.

Fewer and fewer companies control larger and larger chunks of U.S. and global commerce; more than half of the world's largest economies are corporations. Their influence over governments has proceeded apace. In her excellent book *The Silent Takeover: Global Capitalism and the Death of Democracy*, British economist Noreena Hertz writes, "Over the last two years the balance of power between politics and commerce has shifted radically, leaving politicians increasingly subordinate to the colossal economic power of big business. . . . The political state has become the corporate state."

The percentage of total U.S. federal income taxes paid by corporations has steadily decreased; it's not that unusual for a billion-dollar company to pay no income tax at all and even get millions back in rebates. According to Common Cause, seven of America's largest companies received such rebates in 1998. Enron paid no income taxes for four of the five years previous to its bankruptcy, and benefited from having more than nine hundred subsidiaries in overseas tax havens. Ford Motor Company's after-profit tax rate in 2001 ended up being 2.9 percent. Most commercial activity is tax-friendly and heavily subsidized; corporate socialism—or welfare, depending on your point of view—is a fact of life and has been for many years. The slack, of course, is taken up by you and me.

"In 1960, the revenue necessary for the federal budget was divided 40 percent corporations, 40 percent individual, and the remaining 20 percent was from estate taxes and so on," noted a retired tax attorney specializing in tax fraud. "Now the corporation pays approximately 12 percent of the total revenue with the remainder being paid by individuals."

The real wage of the average worker has stagnated or even slipped in recent decades despite increases in the cost-of-living, and two-income families are now the norm. At the same time, executive pay has sky-rocketed. Consider the following progression as charted over time by *Business Week* magazine and summarized in a 1999 report called "A Decade of Executive Excess" by The Institute for Policy Studies and United for a Fair Economy (Exact figures vary somewhat depending on which compensation yardstick is used, e.g., top 100 companies, top 200, etc.):

- It is generally agreed that corporate CEOs made approximately twenty-five times as much in salary as the average hourly production worker in the 1960s.
- In 1988, the average pay of those CEOs had increased to ninety-three times that of "ordinary" workers.
- By the year 2000, top CEOs were making between three hundred and four hundred times as much money per year as you or I. Put another way: Since 1980, the average pay of regular working people increased just 74 percent while CEO pay grew an off-the-chart 1,884 percent!

Worse yet, executive wage inflation has little relationship to corporate performance. For example, the Labor Department reported that even as the Standard & Poor's index dropped 22 percent in 2002, median CEO pay *increased* 22 percent. During the same period, the average worker's salary actually *dropped* 1.5 percent. When profits rebounded in 2003 (up 20 percent according to the Commerce Department, due in no small part to a windfall of new pro-business tax cuts), the money didn't make it very far down the food chain as employee wages managed a paltry 2.8 percent gain (For those who still had a job, anyway. As I write this, a "jobless recovery" is in full swing.).

Not surprisingly, the United States has never been a global leader in economic fairness. In 1980, this country was thirteenth among twenty-two developed nations in what is called "relative equality," a calculation based on income distribution. Today we are dead last, characterized as well (and also not surprisingly) by the highest number of working hours. We are also dead last in overall quality of health. These are hardly encouraging signs that the "American way of life" has no equals. Is this the natural outcome of a "free market" economy driven by individual initiative, or a system rigged for wealth accumulation by the few? I couldn't help but notice that the timeline of wage disparities profiled above coincides roughly with the time period that starts in proximity to the date of the *Business Week* quote that began this chapter: ". . . the idea of doing with less so that big business can have more. . . ."

Many business executives would argue differently, of course. They would claim, for example, that despite the occasional "fluctuation," the economic sea has risen under everyone's boat, domestically and throughout the world; that the average lifespan has never been longer; that literacy and democracy have never been more widespread; that "good" CEOs are hard to find, driving up their prices; that when businesses make money, people have jobs. They would say that global competition keeps everyone from resting easy, and thus the need to create leaner, more efficient operations without the disabling efforts of "unreasonable" legal restraints and grandstanding politicians. Even Bill Gates, founder of Microsoft, once claimed sleepless nights worrying about the next "new, new thing" that could threaten his company's technological dominance.

These claims are not without some merit—few things in this world are wholly evil or angelic, and financially successful businesses are in everyone's best interest. For me, though, it has become a matter not of how much money a company makes but how it makes and distributes it, and corporate power all too often is a one-trick pony.

As I write these pages, the Bush administration and corporate lobbyists are trying to exempt private companies from certain key provisions of the Freedom of Information Act, an audacious play to shield them from public scrutiny. Meanwhile, the Federal Communications Commission voted to allow already giant media companies to expand their influence by pursuing joint ownership of newspapers and television stations in the same city. In a blatant disregard of responsible journalism, this hugely controversial issue was barely covered by the major media—still the primary source of news for most Americans—because, well, the companies that stand to benefit by the FCC decision already own those outlets. Hundreds of thousands of letters from angry citizens had little effect on the Commission. It took a three-judge panel of the Third U.S. Court of Appeals to stay the FCC's; Companies had until January 2005 to file an appeal of the lower court's ruling. The Center for Public Integrity later revealed that FCC employees took twenty-five hundred trips over the previous eight years at a cost of nearly $3 million, largely paid for by these same media companies. The FCC is what government insiders call a "captive agency"—essentially controlled by the industry it was created to regulate. Such corporate/governmental collusion happens with jaw-dropping and dispiriting and under-the-radar regularity.

The ironies are clear enough. In 1776 the framers of the Constitution purposely left out any reference to corporate freedoms or even corporate existence, angered as they were with the heavy-handed actions of their former imperialist masters. The thought that government itself would play such a significant role in corporations' return to power simply didn't exist. And yet we have come full circle—multinationals and other large businesses and industries are once again wielding excessive power, but this time they are the products of our own flawed system.

It's easy to get carried away cataloging the countless incidents of corporate manipulation and misuse of power, and I apologize for my excess. There are plenty of good-guy companies out there—some of which will be profiled later in this book—trying to balance economic and human concerns, and their efforts give me hope. Alas, they're the exception, not the rule. The larger point I've tried to make is that the nature of business often breaks down trust in the workplace and thwarts true meaningfulness because its mission, its very reason for being—maximizing shareholder profit—leaves little room for fuller expressions of our human potential.

We work in an environment where certain rules have been established and we're expected to play by those rules if we want to stay in the game. Changing them seems insurmountable, in part because the target of our discontent seems so vague and undefined. We can take a specific complaint to our supervisor, but how do we confront the flawed character of corporate power? Is it a thing, a person, a name on a piece of paper? Who or what do we point our finger at?

David Korten's conclusion that companies have neither conscience nor soul is a harsh indictment, but the evidence does suggest a frequent absence of moral or ethical judgment when the actions of corporate America are held up to the same standards that you and I as individuals are expected to uphold. Without a social conscience, without a soul or a higher authority than money to answer to, much can be rationalized in the name of profit. As this corporate reality has evolved, so, too, has the workplace that supports it, for it is into this belief system of profit maximization that most daily workers descend, altering themselves to fit the existing culture. That world and its demands have tremendous impacts on how work is structured and which personality types survive best.

CHAPTER 5

The Grip of Corporate Culture

*It is difficult to get a man to understand something when his
salary depends on him not understanding it.*
—UPTON SINCLAIR

W orking with—and for—others can be a fulfilling experience, bringing together such elements as teamwork, recognition, craft, good humor, and monetary reward. When
companies make authentic commitments to maximize the work experience for the people they employ, respecting their individuality while
creating the conditions for positive engagement and creativity, workplace satisfaction improves and so do bottom lines. Unfortunately,
when bottom lines do improve, it's usually not because the work environment of employees has improved but because it has deteriorated,
whether from cuts in benefits or massive layoffs or double workloads
or other profit/efficiency-driven changes. And it seems there is very
little that anyone can do about it.

We generally submit to the purpose of the companies we work for
and how that purpose is carried out without much thought about it.
We have certain talents and skills we wish to use, we need to make a
living using them, there's a legitimate thrill we feel when we work
alongside like-motivated people, and so we look for the best fit we can
find, as do the companies that employ us. Once inside, we go along
to get along. On that level the relationship is relatively straightforward.

But joining a corporate culture is a deceptively significant under-taking, for it will impact how we see ourselves, how we see others, and how we actually behave in a workplace setting. Such cultures discard some of the values we arrive with, reshape others, and add still more. A culture can bring out our best as well as our worst. And yet when we acknowledge the discontent that increasingly characterizes our experience on the job, the depth and breadth of it as evidenced by the data available and the stories we tell ourselves and each other, we can only assume that workplace culture is often a part of the problem.

Are You With Us or Against Us?

A relatively new—and what appears to be a standard—textbook I own called *Organizational Behavior*, synthesizing the writings of several contemporary thinkers on the subject, defines corporate culture as:

> a deeply embedded form of social control that influences employee decisions and behavior. Culture is pervasive and operates uncon-sciously. You might think of it as an automatic pilot, directing employees in ways that are consistent with organizational expec-tations. [It] is the 'social glue' that bonds people together and makes them feel part of the organizational experience. Employees are motivated to internalize the organization's dominant culture because it fulfills their need for social identity.

Despite its acknowledgment of corporate culture's unifying intent, this definition comes across as vaguely ominous: "a form of social con-trol" and "pervasive and operates unconsciously." Sounds more like a kind of Orwellian deception designed to steal our souls. And while a certain amount of control is obviously necessary to achieve a com-pany's mission, the potential for manipulation is clearly evident no matter how "unconscious" the process. In some companies the process isn't unconscious at all. Consider the message on this sign, prominently displayed in a training room at Tyson Foods (which happens to employ a large percentage of foreign workers): "Democracies depend on the political participation of its citizens, but not in the workplace."

Indeed, a more menacing definition of corporate culture is offered by respected scholar Henry Giroux in his book *Impure Acts: The Practical Politics of Cultural Studies*:

> I use the term corporate culture to refer to an ensemble of ideological and institutional forces that function politically and pedagogically to both govern organizational life through senior managerial control and to produce compliant workers, depoliticized consumers, and passive citizens.... Reformulating social issues as strictly individual or economic issues, corporate culture functions largely to cancel out the democratic impulses and practices of civil society by either devaluing them or absorbing such impulses within a market logic. No longer a space for political struggle, culture in the corporate model becomes an all-encompassing horizon for producing market identities, values, and practices.

Giroux's indictment brings to mind the oft-told tale—with its many variations—of the Good Samaritan and the snake, about a man (or a woman or even a child) who responds to the pleas of a poisonous snake in peril, only to be bit after he has taken the reptile to safety. "Why did you do that? I saved your life!" the shocked Samaritan inevitably exclaims. "Well, you knew I was a snake when you picked me up," the snake inevitably replies.

Our workplaces as venomous reptiles? A grim metaphor to consider. But from a particular perspective, it's not hard to imagine that by aligning ourselves with the typical corporate mission—ruled by a financial bottom line—we risk exposure to a potentially toxic value system that prioritizes for behavior inconsistent with a more honorable way of living. In other words, companies can make us do things that—if given the choice—we might not otherwise do, for example, championing a product that may be great for the bottom line but lousy for ecological health, or voting for a candidate who supports your industry but is notoriously unethical on other issues, or working a deal by subtle deceptions, errors of omission, and downright untruths.

Such behavior is inevitable in environments that seek to shape us into reflections of their own images. "The identification of people with their work is a phenomenon that corporations and employers have consciously fostered," writes Sharon Beder in *Selling the Work Ethic*. The objective of such campaigns is to create a kind of *groupthink*—a loyalty-building strategy designed to minimize dissent and maximize conformity. This not entirely unreasonable indoctrination process slowly converts us into card-carrying members (some might say prisoners) of the dominant culture, which we willingly accept because it guarantees a job. We are communal creatures by nature—Western individualism notwithstanding—and work remains our primary measurement of self-worth. (How good do *you* feel about yourself when you don't have a job?) Our critical faculties may be asked to yield to the company line, but do it enough times and the surrender becomes second nature. Not doing so can jeopardize one's economic future, and certainly any progression up the corporate ladder.

I don't mean to imply that such "sell-outs" are the norm, only to point out that this tendency to give in seems the inevitable outcome of a system that prioritizes for and sometimes even demands conformity. Discussing the powerful influence that the tobacco industry culture has on those who work within it, John Dalla Costa, in his book *The Ethical Imperative: Why Moral Leadership Is Good Business*, muses:

> Why would tobacco CEOs stand before the U.S. Congress and risk perjury, the ignominy of jail and the opprobrium of history to lie about the addictiveness and health dangers of smoking? . . . Operating by their own code has given tobacco companies the

fortitude to fight long battles with governments, special interest groups and world public opinion. Groups construct their own principles, and sometimes those principles are lies: in the case of the tobacco companies it is the crusade to protect free speech and sell their legal product. Amazingly, such principles have cogency and are compelling to members of the group, even when the group's norms are by historical, social, and religious norms heinous and indefensible. So strong is this hold on the moral imagination of the group that defectors are made pariahs, even if defectors are right by society's moral standard. . . . To the group, being loyal is more important than being right.

This dynamic is similar to the black-and-white realities of our military institutions and certain party politics. You're either with us or against us—there is no middle ground. Sometimes that's the way it needs to be; there will always be issues where sharp lines must be drawn. At the same time, the middle ground—the realm of "I don't know what is truly best for all"—can be a fertile area for discovering insights that, instead of serving the interests of specific agendas, contribute to more egalitarian, and often wiser, solutions. One must be open to such discoveries, willing to step outside the boundaries of designated roles to pursue larger truths. Often we are not, unwilling to take the risk. There is a saying in Japan, long a culture of conformity, that the protruding nail gets hammered. Who wants to get bonked on the head?

In the novel *Moral Hazard*, Kate Jennings places her protagonist in the heartless center of the New York City investment world where she works as a speechwriter to help support a husband she is slowly losing to Alzheimer's. Wary at first, she finally makes peace with the obfuscating intent of her efforts, only to finally break down under the weight of too many rationalizations that serve cold-blooded objectives. "Corporations are like fortressed city-states," she declares to her uncomprehending husband one day on an outing to a small café.

Or occupied territories. Remember *The Sorrow and the Pity?* Nazi-occupied France, the Vichy government? Remember the way people rationalized their behavior, cheering Petain at the beginning and then cheering de Gaulle at the end? In corporations, there are out-and-out collaborators. Opportunists. Born that way. But most of the employees are like the French in the forties. Fearful. *Attentiste.* Waiting to see what happens. Hunkering down. Turning a blind eye.

Even as we fear for our professional lives, we are caught in a web that we aren't sure we want to escape from. The influence of workplace culture is deceptively strong. As it takes up more and more of our time, it becomes our surrogate family, community, even lover, satisfying more and more of our emotional and social needs in ways that aren't always healthy. Summarizing the message of Arlie Hochschild's *The Time Bind: When Work Becomes Home and Home Becomes Work*, a reviewer in the *Utne Reader* wrote:

> [E]ven when a company offers flexible policies, most employees don't take advantage of them—and not just because they're worried about layoffs or are strapped for cash. At least for middle-class professionals, work has become the source of rewards, emotional support, friendships, community feeling. More disturbing, they tend to buy into the workaholic pace, blaming themselves or family obligations—instead of managers who expect ever-higher productivity—if they can't keep up.

The author of an article in *Modern Maturity* magazine about the relentlessness of work revealed that "When I interviewed 40 men about their work-life tradeoffs, every one of them said that it was easier to be a success on the job than in his personal relationship."

The schizophrenic realtionships we have with our jobs—equal parts sanctuary and bastille—is in large part a product of our own inner wiring. The values and characteristics that are *primarily* emphasized in business—hierarchy, competition, efficiency, team work, advancement—are already active in each individual psyche. We have become so accustomed to equating individual progress with material gain that it's no great leap from our personal life to our work life. We are trained to be acquisitive and materialistic, we live in a county where individualism and personal initiative is a creed, and a corporate mindset has evolved where these forces are very much at play. Corporate self-interest and personal self-interest have thus formed a natural partnership in pursuit of economic gain. From a purely materialistic point of view the results have been impressive (though no longer guaranteed). From a broader social, cultural, and environmental perspective, however, and from the standpoint of our own precarious states of physical health, the benefits have been much less obvious.

The Disenchanted Workplace

In chapter 3, I cited a number of studies showing that our culture of materialism and overwork has taken a toll on everyday Americans. In the workplace are similar signs that all is not well, whether you work for a globalizing multinational or in the "middle kingdom" where most other businesses reside. Corporate cultures hardwired for profit, using organizational models still heavily influenced by a mechanistic paradigm of how and why people work, are causing many to rethink their loyalties.

Employees—real people—are routinely referred to as human capital, intangible assets, part of a knowledge base to be leveraged or liabilities to be discarded. Such a depersonalized approach to management is natural within the mechanistic model that most companies follow. A recently popularized management tool called "forced ranking," for example, plots employees along a bell curve and assigns them a letter grade: 10 percent are given As, 10 percent are Cs (the at-risk group), and the remaining 80 percent are Bs. And what if there are no Cs in a company? Well, forced ranking will find some, even if it has to make them up! (Other such systems use a 1–4 or other numerical form of ranking.) The result is that employees may start to compete with each other, such as withholding information or politicking behind someone's back. Personality conflicts with a difficult manager can lower one's ranking. Companies that have forced ranking have been accused of using it as an easy way to justify job cuts or reallocate benefits ("rank and yank"). All of this can have a destabilizing impact on a workforce.

Nearly half of the respondents in a 2004 survey of human resource professionals conducted by Equation Research and sponsored by Novations Group, Inc., felt that their company's forced ranking system damaged morale, reduced collaboration and teamwork, and generated mistrust of leadership. Yes, there need to be methods of assessment that protect companies from underperforming employees, but such approaches as forced ranking take the humanity out of the process, which is the very thing that is already lacking.

Indeed, in the spirit of Descartes, the maxim "Just like clockwork" has become the prevailing mantra at work. A *Business Week* article notes "Face time at the office has become increasingly irrelevant in climbing the corporate ladder. Instead, output and productivity are the gauges of success." Feelings are inappropriate; results are everything. That's the hope, anyway, among the executive elite, but the two cannot be so easily separated. In fact, the way we *feel* about our jobs has tremendous impact on workplace satisfaction and performance.

The findings of a recent study called "Working Today: Exploring Employee's Emotional Connection to Their Jobs" (referred to earlier in the book) seem especially revealing. The study surveyed a randomly selected group of eleven hundred employees working for mid-sized to large companies across the United States and Canada. The respondents were asked to describe how they felt about both their current jobs and an "ideal" work experience. At the same time, three hundred senior human resource executives (one-third Canadian) from those same companies were asked how *they* thought their employees would describe their current work experience. Survey results turned out to be similar in both countries. Among the more significant findings:

- More than half of all respondents reported having negative feelings about their jobs; one-third described those feelings as "intensely negative."
- More than one-quarter of those in the "intensely negative" group are actively looking for other work, compared to only 6 percent of those with positive feelings about their work. A similar percentage of those with negative feelings plan to stay in their jobs—a ticking bomb of disaffection and poor performance.
- There was a significant difference between how respondents described their current jobs and how they envisioned an ideal work experience.
- A five-year analysis of shareholder returns found a strong correlation between satisfied employees and corporate performance.

The most telling statistic of yet another workplace survey carried out by an individual company was that only 42 percent of its employees felt that senior management had a sincere interest in their well-being. In a related study by the same company, nearly 80 percent said they were satisfied with their work but 52 percent disagreed with the statement that their company showed care and concern for its workers. It's no surprise that researchers are discovering a lack in the workplace of what one company called "*engagement*—employees' willingness and ability to contribute to company success, [which] ultimately comes down to people's willingness to give discretionary effort in their jobs."

In my book *Communication Miracles at Work*, I cited the results of a 1994 "workplace-values" survey in which the majority of respondents preferred to be motivated by management techniques based on caring and wanted more freedom to express their feelings. What they reported were corporations that tended to use fear to motivate and which felt that feelings had no place in the office. How much of that has changed? Well, a much more recent study (2003) by management consultant Franklin Covey found that just 31 percent of 11,045 employees surveyed felt they could express themselves honestly and candidly at work. If this is true, it means that seven out of ten people you work with are unwilling to tell the full truth about a situation because they fear what will happen if they do! Perhaps even more startling: Only 9 percent believed that their work had a strong link to their organization's top priorities—a serious case of disconnect and alienation.

The real workforce in any company—let's call them the "Bs" of a forced ranking system—are considered the most disenfranchised, seeing themselves as overworked and taken for granted. "People are so undervalued here—we feel like commodities," said one software engineer quoted in a *Time* magazine article. They are also the most likely to leave when—and if—the economy takes off again, especially if all of these surveys showing high levels of discontent can be believed. And while opportunism will be part of their motivation, disgust with how they're treated and with the policies of their employers will no doubt share the blame.

It would be easy for upper management to overlook such signs; you can't please all employees all the time, and workplace discontent is hardly a new phenomena. But such disregard would be foolhardy; something isn't working, and the fallout is insidious. The only conclusion one can draw from these results is that too many companies are doing a poor job of creating a workplace culture in which employees feel comfortable enough to be themselves and do their best.

Try to recall your latest job interview or, if you were on the other side of the table, the interview you conducted with a prospective employee. What kinds of questions were asked? Job skills? Industry knowledge? Greatest strengths and weaknesses? It's important, of course, that companies find qualified people who understand their business and have the right experience to further the corporate mission. But has anyone ever asked how important is it to treat others with respect, or what management's responsibility is to make a workplace humane, or what a company's role should be in addressing social or environmental issues? Not likely.

If the places we work have neither a soul nor a conscience, then what do we to do with ours when we walk in the door? What has to change for us to feel reconnected with our work? As Matthew Fox wrote in *The Reinvention of Work*, "If we are not being served truth and justice as regular fare at work, then no matter how well we are fed materially, we will starve spiritually. Our work must make way for the heart . . . all the promotions and fat paychecks in the world will not assuage the feeling that we are dying in the soul."

This is why I decided to write candidly in this and the previous two chapters about what I felt was wrong with the system, which essentially boils down to the fact that overworked, stressed-out men and women living beyond their means must rely on—and are thus vulnerable to—companies that often care more about making money than serving the needs of those who help them make it. For me it has felt like putting on an ill-fitting suit; I have some movement but I can never get my arms over my head or bend my knees without risking a split seam. The result: a kind of rigidity that seems to limit our choices when forced to deal with difficult situations involving coworkers or management. The dynamics of those choices, and the sometimes blurry lines between our employer's agenda and our personal agenda, are explored in depth in the following chapter.

CHAPTER 6

Personal Values and Corporate Mind

*It is likely that the majority of people in the work force will
continue to be caught in the struggle for survival, and that they
will make their subliminal deals for material success and
security.*
　　—LET DAVIDSON, *Wisdom at Work*

Chained to a relentless work ethic, constrained by corporate cultures designed to keep us in line, it's no wonder that an enlightened approach to our livelihood seems so out of reach. Complicated forces shape our workplace identities and the decisions we make and limit our view of what work can and should be. How do we balance our own personal values with corporate ones? How can we stay true to ourselves while appeasing workplace gods?

For many of us, money still trumps meaning when it comes to what we're willing to live with and give up. We have inherited a system that meets certain undeniable needs as long as we accept the values and ethics that go along with it. This we have done, wittingly or not, and in return given up some of the "softer" qualities of humanness that sustain us on a different level. Some of those qualities are as simple as courtesy and kindness; others have to do with trust and respect.

Over time, the loss of this connective tissue, this glue of our common humanity, can be emotionally damaging: cynicism, unhappiness, despair, or a cocktail of more than one. These feelings may not be immediately obvious, but if we look closely at our experience at work, at how we feel at the end of the day or when we first get up in the morning, if we scratch just below the surface of our concessions, we may find a more unsettling reality. It's hardly the outcome we deserve for the enormous commitments we make to our jobs. And yet in a techno/global economy where capital is mobile and people are expendable, survival concerns are never more than a paycheck or two away. Pushed by the uncertainty of our economic lives, we thus trudge stoically forward, clinging to the jobs we have, desperately searching for those we don't, all the while thirsting for drops of meaning and purpose that don't derive solely from an economic well.

The Problem with Self-Interest

The struggle to retain our humanness at work is handicapped not only by the need to survive but also the conditioning that equates more with better and money with success. "Growth is good" is the American economy's holy grail, whether it's moving up a corporate ladder or expanding market share or simply having more money in your pocket at the end of the day. These are not necessarily bad things, but when "progress" doesn't include inner-directed goals or concern for the well-being of the world outside you, then I don't think you can call it progress. It is more like the satisfaction of narrow self-interest, be it corporate or individual, and that is no ally to finding meaningfulness at work unless your definition of meaningful is quite narrow.

And so as much as I enjoy indicting the motives of corporate America, I have a hard time separating them from the ones that characterize those with a personal financial stake in its success. I'm referring to owners and executives, of course, but also to anyone who owns a share of stock or receives a weekly paycheck—anyone, that is, who depends on the system for their economic survival. In short, you and me.

Over the years I've had numerous conversations with family and friends about whether they'd be just as happy with a lower "return on investment" if the companies they invested in adhered to higher social or environmental standards. The answer, more often than not, has been a disappointing "no." It doesn't help that such celebrity financial consultants as Suze Orman advise people to invest their money in presumably higher-returning traditional funds and then donate any difference (assuming, of course, that there is one) to more "charitable" causes. Who actually does this? "Enlightened" shareholder resolutions (translation: those that address issues not directly designed to bolster the bottom line) always face an uphill struggle. In a recent example, resolutions challenging Exxon Mobile on global warming, corporate accountability, and human rights were soundly defeated at the company's 2002 annual meeting, much of the muscle—but not all—provided by a minority of major stockholders.

Both people and companies have become programmed over the years to consider the value of business and investment solely through the lens of an economic payoff. This tacit complicity has created some uncomfortable ironies. In an article for *Salon.com* entitled "Wall Street Echoes," political columnist Arianna Huffington took the public to task for shaking its collective head at the notorious actions of Enron's Jeff Skilling and other criminally negligent CEOs, suggesting that we have sometimes allowed—and even abetted—such outcomes:

> [B]efore we get too comfortable—and self-righteous—pointing our Monday morning fingers at these white-collar crooks without a conscience, we need to admit that their antisocial behavior couldn't have flourished in a vacuum. We allowed it. Even celebrated it. . . . During the '90s, denial replaced baseball as the national pastime. We buried our heads in the sand—unwilling to question the integrity of the bulls rushing down Wall Street for fear it might jeopardize the 30 percent rate of return we had come to see as our birthright. . . . [These CEOs] were nothing more

than the winners of a game we all wanted to play—a game that we knew rewarded certain aberrant behaviors.

There has long been an economic maxim that selfishness is good, that if everyone followed their own self-interest then all the needs of society would be met in the great open marketplace of ideas and initiative and debate and personal choice. I can certainly relate to the power of selfishness as a motivator for action, but as an unchallenged force for good, I'm far less convinced. In a world so interconnected and inter-related as ours, putting our own needs ahead of all else—needs that may be distorted by the kind of society we live in—does not usually lead to the greatest common good, which I believe is the ultimate measure of the wisdom of one's intent. As this book has suggested (by no means an original hypothesis), the entanglement of narrow self-interests, personal and corporate, that is as much conscious as unconscious, is leading us down a dangerous path.

This alliance was taken to extremes in the case of Enron and other corporate giants who recently succumbed to years of gross dishonesty and deceit, but the devilish essence of it can operate at many levels. As Chris Seay writes in *The Tao of Enron*:

> When capitalism unwittingly marries unbridled Western indi-vidualism . . . every person creates a society for himself and her-self, thus making a mockery of the idea of a nation of liberty and freedom. The thinking [in what he calls "the fatal flaw in the Western world"] goes something like this: If in my freedom I make choices based solely on profit—even if those choices devastate the lives of hundreds or even thousands of people—I shouldn't feel guilty. It's my right, and it's the American way.

In questioning the power of money over our lives, Seay's frustra-tion is not out of line. And while the motives of the majority of us are saintly compared to the immoral intent of those pilloried executives, we are vulnerable nevertheless.

I'm as guilty as anyone for buying into the mind-set that more is better and the rest of the world will take care of itself. I tell myself that I'm not, but the record suggests otherwise: I don't give enough to charity; I don't often stand up to those who misuse power; I've willingly worked for companies whose services helped others defile the environment. In myriad small ways, I've allowed my choices to reflect not the person I want to be but the one I am—a survivalist, always adapting to my circumstances, rationalizing the tradeoffs. There is a saying that goes something like, "It's the things we let ourselves get away with that define the character of our lives and the world we live in."

"Why do greed and selfishness command such a following?" ask Denise Breton and Christopher Largent in *The Soul of Economies*. "Not because we're necessarily that greedy, but because we believe . . . that these responses reflect the realities of economic life. In the end, we think either that greed can't be restrained, or that without it economies would fizzle. The root is philosophical: we take greed and selfishness to be what economies are all about."

There are many who point the finger at Adam Smith as sanctioning the glory of self-interest, but a careful reading of his work—not just *The Wealth of Nations* but its precursor, *The Theory of Moral Sentiments*—suggests no such endorsement, as numerous scholars and authorities have concluded. In fact, Smith apparently took great pains to warn against economic concentration and unregulated greed, distrusted big government *and* big companies, and wrote in the very beginning of his book, "How selfish soever man may be supposed, there are evidently some principles in his nature, which interest him in the fortune of others, and render their happiness necessary to him, though he derives nothing from it, except the pleasure of seeing it." In other words, a person's own contentment depends in large part on ensuring the contentment of others.

The Decisions That Define Us

Although the pursuit of money and the options it provides makes sense in this materialistic world, that pursuit often forces decisions and compromises that conflict with deeper parts of us. All too often we ignore those pleas and bend ourselves toward existing workplace dogma whether or not it mirrors our own. After a while those standards are internalized, and whatever high-minded ideals we may have arrived with soon fall victim to the demands of the job, whatever our position may be. Those demands often leave little room for ethical ruminations on the wisdom of our choices; once we've entered the corporate world we are swept up in the strong current of its urgencies. We may want to be different at work, we would like nothing better than to behave honorably and compassionately and infuse our work with meaning, but the reality often presents us with difficult choices. Our principles and resolve are tested in the day-to-day decisions we make.

Ed Petry, executive director of the Ethics Officer Association, admits that achieving a balance between pursuit of profit and moral responsibility is "one of the biggest obstacles that ethics officers struggle with. You do have short-term pressures and it affects everyone in the company. Even good people who want to do the right thing are going to be tempted to cross the line."

In *Tyranny of the Bottom Line: Why Corporations Make Good People Do Bad Things*, Ralph Estes writes:

> Today managers may be told to promote good corporate citizenship, to not discriminate or pollute or harm customers, but all managers know that ultimately they are judged primarily on a single dimension—the bottom line. If it is not high enough, all their good intentions and good deeds may be for naught. Indeed they may be out of a job. So in weighing day-to-day decisions, managers' internal, personal morality and good intentions will, too many times, give way to actions that may be harmful to stake-

holders but promise to raise the bottom line. This doesn't mean they are evil people. It means they are in the clutches of a performance evaluation system, a scorekeeping system, that was never designed to account for [anything but profit].

Problems arise when our individual instincts get tired of colliding with the imperatives of the collective, when personal values start conflicting with corporate goals. It may be a clear case of right vs. wrong, as someone like Jeffrey Wigand faced when deciding to confront tobacco industry deceptions; wrong vs. right, as WorldCom executives may briefly have considered before fleecing taxpayers and shareholders; or murkier instances of "right vs. right," as Joseph Badaracco describes in his excellent book *Defining Moments: When Managers Must Choose between Right and Right.*

Typical of these was the dilemma faced by bank manager Rebecca Dennet when informed by her supervisor that her branch would shut down in two months—near the first of the year—and told to keep the news confidential. "Two days later," Badaracco writes, "a coworker [and good friend] asked Dennet if she knew anything about the rumor that the branch would soon be closed. When she hesitated, the coworker grew impatient and said, 'Look, this is serious. There aren't a lot of jobs around here. Do I cut back on Christmas gifts?'" What would you have done in Dennet's shoes? How would your decision have defined you? If you told your friend, would it have been out of spite for the company or because you truly thought it was the fair thing to do? If you didn't tell your friend, would it have been out of fear of reprisal from your supervisor or because you agreed with your employer's logic?

When self-interest and corporate interest are in alignment—even if that interest is devoted to ruthless conquest—there are few ethical or emotional challenges and the work experience proceeds with little conflict. When those interests diverge, the accumulated stress of ignoring your own sense of right and wrong or even comfort and discomfort can start bearing down with an unendurable weight. We start to feel more aware of and less okay with the tradeoffs we have made; there aren't enough psychological or even spiritual payoffs. We become alienated from what our work could be under a different set of principles and priorities, the situation now ripe with discontent. Badaracco speaks primarily of the dilemmas faced by managers who are in unique positions to influence company direction, but the nucleus of the conflicts he describes confronts anyone who works in corporate America, no matter the size of the company.

Ethical issues have never had a prominent place in business or in the universities that train us for business careers. They are too difficult to sort out, too risky to consider when money or expediency are at stake, too messy in a world that wants its answers FedEx'd in nice square boxes. In a 2002 *Washington Post* editorial titled "Where Have All the Values Gone?," Amitai Etzioni, a scholar and leading intellectual on morality and values, recounted his experiences as an ethics professor at Harvard Business School in the late eighties:

> [T]he chairman of the SEC made a personal donation of $20 million to HBS to support the teaching of ethics. After months of contentious debate, an initial proposal was put up for a faculty vote. . . . Reactions ranged from distrust to outright hostility. One economist argued that "We are here to teach science." Another faculty member wanted to know, "Whose ethics, what values, are we going to teach?" And a third pointed out that the students were adults who got their ethics education at home and at church. By meeting's end, the project had been sent back to the drawing board.
>
> Debates continued over whether ethics should be a required course or a separate elective or, alternatively, whether the topic should be integrated into all classes. A member of the marketing department mused that if the policy ethics in all classes were adopted, his department would have to close because much of

what it was teaching constituted a form of dissembling: selling small items in large boxes, putting hot colors on packages because they encouraged people to buy impulsively, and so forth. . . .

In my own HBS ethics classes students resisted my argument that executives should consider ethics. They held, as they had been taught, that a company focused on efficiency would drive a second one, more concerned with ethics, out of business. Ethics, they told me repeatedly, were something a corporation simply cannot afford.

Even in a post-Enron world, change has been slow to come. A recent Aspen Institute study tracked the attitudes of MBA students over the course of their education and found that at the beginning of their program, 67 percent believed that maximizing shareholder values was the prime responsibility of a company. By the end of their first year that figure had *increased* to 82 percent. In early 2003, the Association to Advance Collegiate Schools of Business—a St. Louis-based group that accredits most U.S. business schools—proposed new standards urging colleges to make teaching ethics a higher priority but decided not to recommend that such classes become part of required curriculum.

At the same time, there are signs of hope. The Aspen Institute also conducts an ongoing study called "Beyond Grey Pinstripes" that tracks the growth of business school coursework devoted to social and environmental issues. The results for 2003 showed that 45 percent of 188 responding schools (out of 560 contacted), including many of the top business schools in the country, required students to take one or more courses on such subjects as ethics, corporate social responsibility, and sustainability—how a company can meet its financial goals while having a neutral impact on the environment. That compares to 34 percent of schools in 2001 and less than 30 percent in the 2000 survey. And a 2004 study by Stanford and University of California, Santa Barbara, found that the majority of the 800 MBA students it surveyed *said* they would accept a lower salary to work with a company that was considered ethical and socially reponsible.

$$\sim$$

Issues of ethics and self-interest are important subsets of the larger challenge to find meaning in the work we do. Whether it's the work itself, the management we labor under, the culture that controls us, or concerns about our future, we are faced with decisions every day that cumulatively define who we are and how we feel about what we do. These decisions have to do with the policies we support, how we treat coworkers and clients, the best ways to lead, and how to achieve our personal goals. Even as some companies try to create values-centered environments based on honesty, respect, fairness, and so on, most workplaces challenge us to fight for those very things. Often we respond out of ignorance or fear, unaware of our options, afraid to stand up for the principles we believe in. We choose not to be the protruding nail.

Breaking free from the constraints that bind us to old ways of approaching work is a struggle that everyone faces. The goals we have, the values that motivate us, the responsibilities we bear, the companies we work for, the society we live in—each has a role in that process. To transform the workplace we need to make wiser and more courageous decisions while seeking to understand why and how we continue making wrong ones.

Thankfully there are ways to bring more awareness to our jobs and to their purpose in our lives while respecting the realities that confront us. This journey of self-transformation relies on faith, desire, and action to create new patterns of thinking and behavior. Faith is the belief that our efforts will be worthwhile. Desire reflects a commitment to change. Action brings that change into reality. It's a process that evolves one decision at a time. By educating ourselves and taking new risks, we forge new paths toward wisdom.

A growing number of visionary and compassionate and practical people and the organizations they work for are doing just that, forging new trails to remake commerce into a more reliable force for good. Their actions may not always bring overnight change, and indeed the structural flaws in the system and in our psyches may take years and perhaps generations to undo, but they are proving that positive change *and* financial achievement are not only possible but everyday realities.

PART 3

The Practice: A Path for companies

CHAPTER 7

The Emergence of Corporate Integrity

*My point, and most basic argument, is that the [free market]
economy is a wonderful invention, but it must be managed as
an instrument of humanity, and never the other way around.*
——JOHN DALLA COSTA, *The Ethical Imperative: Why Moral
Leadership Is Good Business*

A s a working stiff I have always been keenly aware that the
"business of America" has shown little interest in the kinds of
policies whose benefits cannot easily be quantified. Good corporate citizenship, socially responsible business, fair and humane workplaces—these ideas have remained largely outside executive radar. As
many decision-makers are quick to admit, "If you can't measure it, you
can't manage it," giving them reason enough to keep such initiatives off
their to-do lists. The scandals of the last several years, however, and
the cumulative discontent that now characterizes so many workplaces,
have given these notions new legitimacy.

Even *Business Week* magazine acknowledged that new corporate
models are necessary and inevitable. In the post-Enron world, they
write:

corporations will likely become far more transparent—not only for
investors, but also for employees, customers, and suppliers. The
single-minded focus on "shareholder value," which measured performance on the sole basis of stock price, will diminish. Instead,

companies will elevate the interests of employees, customers, and their communities. Executive pay, which clearly soared out of control in the past two decades, is already undergoing a reassessment and will likely fall back in an effort to create a sense of fairness. And corporate cultures will change in a way that puts greater emphasis on integrity and trust.

Yes, megalithic multinationals still march largely unimpeded across the global economic landscape, and "dominator" models of relationship and organization—hierarchical, competitive, controlling—still far outnumber partnership models. But despite what the headlines suggest, more and more companies are quietly stepping up to meet the challenges. Corporate leaders, motivated to renew their company's mission as well as their own personal purpose, are taking their businesses in new directions. Everything from childcare and flextime to management teams, community service, environmental activism, and even contemplative practice have turned certain companies into places that people are proud to work for, inspiring loyalty that can't be purchased by a paycheck alone. Some are responding to outside pressures, others to a workforce newly excited by the possibilities that work can offer, and still others to their own growing desire to make a positive difference in the world—the reason doesn't matter so long as the shift is genuine.

In *Values Shift: The New Work Ethic and What It Means for Business*, authors John Izzo and Pam Withers profile dozens of companies that made authentic commitments to building humane workplaces and serving the interests of all their stakeholder groups. *Good to Great: Why Some Companies Make the Leap and Others Don't* by Jim Collins and *Built to Last: Successful Habits of Visionary Companies,* by Collins and Jerry Porras, spent months on business bestseller lists. One of their main findings? That "maximizing shareholder wealth" is not the driving force behind the most successful and enduring companies. Instead, the main engine is a "core ideology" that sees beyond the strictly monetary. Another discovery? That humility, not ego, characterizes the most effective leaders.

The Numerous Benefits of Principled Business

The clearest expression of how a transformed corporate America would look on the operational ground floor can be found in the principles of what has come to be called the "corporate social responsibility" (CSR) movement, defined by the membership organization Business for Social Responsibility (BSR) as "achieving commercial success in ways that honor ethical values and respect people, communities, and the natural environment . . . addressing the legal, ethical, commercial and other expectations society has for business, and making decisions that fairly balance the claims of all key stakeholders." In short, CSR is a way for companies that insist on the rights of personhood to rehabilitate themselves into more responsible corporate citizens, accountable to certain standards.

Up to now, most companies have scoffed at such potential redeployment of resources and reshuffling of priorities, primarily out of fear and ignorance. Swept up in old ways of doing business, they fear loss of control and constraints on profit making yet know little about what such redirection could do for them. A growing number of others, however, are converting; some are even reengineering their entire corporate structure. Numerous organizations and awards programs in the United States are devoted to supporting more intelligent and sensitive business practices and honoring socially and environmentally responsible performance. Sensitive to the need to justify such policies in concrete terms, CSR advocates have been tracking their impact for years. The surprising result is that the benefits of truly following the principles of CSR practice are numerous and tangible, as exhaustively documented on the BSR Web site (www.bsr.org):

- **Improved financial performance.** The most recent evidence for this is a study done by DePaul University comparing *Business Ethics* magazine's Top 100 Corporate Citizens in 2001 to S&P 500 companies that didn't make the list. According to professor Curtis C. Verschoor, who codirected the study, "Overall financial performance of the 2001 *Business Ethics* Best Citizen companies was significantly better than that of the remaining companies in the S&P 500 index, based on the 2001 *Business Week* ranking of total financial performance." A similar study in the United Kingdom over a recent five-year period found a positive correlation between companies with an ethics code and superior financial performance.

- **Increased sales and customer loyalty.** Beyond satisfying basic consumer demands regarding "price, quality, availability, safety and convenience," companies are finding their sales affected by how customers and potential customers perceive them on a qualitative basis: Can this company be trusted? Are they doing good things in the world (or not doing bad things)? BSR cited two recent studies suggesting that a company's corporate citizenship profile directly affects buying decisions:

  1. A 2001 Hill & Knowlton/Harris Interactive poll showed that 79 percent of Americans take corporate citizenship into account when deciding whether to buy a particular company's product; 36 percent of Americans consider corporate citizenship an important factor when making purchasing decisions.
  2. A 2002 Cone Corporate Citizenship Study found that 91 percent of those surveyed would consider switching to another company if they learned of a firm's negative corporate citizenship practices. Eighty-five percent would pass the information to family and friends, 83 percent

would refuse to invest in that company, 80 percent would refuse to work at that company, and 76 percent would boycott that company's products.

- **Enhanced brand image and reputation.** A 2001 poll that asked more than twenty-five thousand people worldwide to name the factors that most influenced how they felt about a particular company found labor practices, business ethics, social responsibility, and environmental impact to be the most frequently cited. Traditional measures of business fundamentals such as revenue growth, strategy, management, and so on turned out to be far less important.

- **Reduced regulatory oversight.** There are a variety of federal and state programs that recognize and reward companies for taking proactive measures to reduce environmental, health, and safety hazards. In many cases, such companies are subject to fewer inspections and paperwork, and may be given preference or "fast-track" treatment when applying for operating permits, zoning variances, or other forms of governmental permission. U.S. Federal Sentencing Guidelines allow penalties and fines against corporations to be reduced or even eliminated if a company can show it has taken "good corporate citizenship" actions and has an effective ethics program in place.

- **Access to Capital.** Socially Responsible Investing (SRI) remains a growth industry despite difficult economic times, spurred by continued disenchantment with traditional institutions of investment and an authentic desire to support companies committed to making a positive difference in the world. According to the Social Investment Forums 2003 biannual report, "socially screened" portfolios increased over 1100% between 1995 and 2003, compared to 174% growth in non-screened asset management during the same period. This growth, says BSR, "means companies with strong CSR performance have increased access to capital that might not otherwise have been available." It should be noted, though, that a typical SRI portfolio will not look much different from a list of Dow Jones stocks—the definition of SRI has broadened considerably.

- **Other benefits.** These can include lower operating costs, higher productivity, improved product quality, and lower rates of absenteeism when workers believe in their employer's mission and feel supported by corporate policy (e.g., greater employee autonomy and work/life programs such as flexible scheduling, job sharing, child care, and "healthy worker" incentives). Not surprisingly, such companies have little trouble attracting and retaining employees. Those on the *Business Ethics* Top 100 list, for example, receive twice as many job applications as their competitors and claim half the turnover rate.

Worldwide, sustainability advocacy is on the rise as well, typified by the work of Global Compact, launched by United Nations secretary-general Kofi Annan in 2000. According to GC's 2002 Annual Report, more than one thousand companies from fourteen countries are participating in this corporate citizenship initiative, which presents nine principles for corporate action to help business leaders integrate environmental and social justice values into their operations. In addition, the theme of the 2003 World Economic Forum, not usually a hotbed of corporate accountability issues, was "Building Trust," an obvious response to the ethical scandals that have rocked the workplace. Even The Conference Board, a longtime business support group, responded to the outcry over lapsed business judgments with calls to overhaul corporate behavior standards, institute corporate sustainability reporting, and "resist the temptation to waive [such commitments] when times are hard."

Stronger Medicine for Corporate Change

With so much evidence that "good works" pay off—at many levels—
and in light of a belief in the natural inclination of people to do the
right thing, it's still a wonder that more companies aren't taking stock
of themselves and turning in a more conscious direction. This idea is
certainly not lost on a public increasingly wary of the corporate wealth
machine. In a 2000 *Business Week* poll, a staggering 95 percent of
respondents felt that corporations should "sacrifice some profit for the
sake of making things better for their workers and communities." An
easy sentiment to support in the abstract, and yet the nearly unani-
mous agreement across a wide section of beliefs and values suggests a
sea change in thinking among a population hungry for a dose of
corporate integrity.

But as we saw in part 2, there are powerful forces at work—individual and institutional—undermining the will to change course. As
Frederick Douglass, a former slave who became an influential voice in
the abolitionist movement and an advisor to President Lincoln, once
said, "Neither charm nor patience nor endurance has ever wrested
power from those who hold it." And with the stakes so high and getting
higher, can we trust that good faith efforts will be enough to convince
business to change its ways?

If the voluntary efforts mentioned above are the carrot, then the stick
would be measures that *require* corporate behavior to change. Such
intervention is anathema to the spirit—and most current law—of
Western capitalism, but there are some who feel that stronger medi-
cine is needed to rid our businesses of this disease called profit
maximization.

"Enron rang all the bells of CSR," Marjorie Kelly wrote in the
May/June 2002 issue of *Business Ethics*.

> It won a spot for three years on the list of the 100 Best Companies
> to Work for in America. In 2000 it received six environmental

awards. It issued a triple bottom line report. It had great policies on climate change, human rights, and (yes, indeed) anti-corruption. Its CEO gave speeches at ethics conferences and put together a statement of values emphasizing "communication, respect, and integrity." The company's stock was in many social investing mutual funds when it went down.

This is happening even at the "best" firms. I've had candid conversations with managers at top-tier firms among our 100 Best Corporate Citizens, and what I hear is disheartening. One executive with her firm 18 years told me recently, "I'm inside the most enlightened company, and I'm telling you, it is no more . . . . What's going on is a single thing: unremitting pressure to get the numbers, by any means possible."

Addressing these concerns and the mechanisms behind them is the mission of numerous activist groups and individuals who don't have the patience for voluntary initiatives and who prefer to see some teeth behind incentives to make corporations more humane and accountable. Most of their suggestions are legislatively inspired, such as Robert Hinkley's proposed twenty-eight-word governance clause that acknowledges corporate directors' responsibility to carry out their duties in good faith, "but not at the expense of the environment, human rights, the public health or safety, the communities in which the corporation operates or the dignity of its employees." Another is the Code for Corporate Responsibility (*www.citizenWorks.org*), which lays out its case for putting the brakes on profit making with a preamble and ten sections that are both principled and punitive. Two states, California and Minnesota, currently have bills in their legislature that would change the language in their corporate charters in such a fashion. POCLAD, the Program on Corporations, Law, and Democracy, discredits the very notion of corporate personhood/citizenship, and is dedicated to "instigating democratic conversation and actions" that challenge corporate authority and control.

Following are some of the most frequently cited ideas for reigning in corporate power and building sustainability into normal business practice:

- Require boards of directors to be diverse and to contain members who are independently elected.
- Give employees a stronger voice in corporate governance, such as seats on boards of directors.
- Minimize consolidation of power by separating the roles of Chairman and CEO.
- Make it easier for individuals to prove that a company damaged the "public interest" and to sue for personal harm done.
- Expense employee stock options, which basically means that a company must claim immediately as an expense any options granted in lieu of salary.
- Link executive pay to profits rather than share price, and to "measurable" progress on issues of corporate responsibility.
- Give shareholders more voice in corporate affairs and make simple majority-rule resolutions binding (instead of the "supermajority" requirements currently in force).
- Require that companies of a certain size go through a rechartering/review process every x number of years.
- Prevent government contracts from being awarded to companies with a history of civil or criminal violations.
- Increase penalties for white-collar crime.
- Mandate deeper, wider, and more clearly written disclosure reporting and ensure distribution to all relevant stakeholders.
- Stop the industry/regulator revolving door by requiring more diversity and independence (e.g., noncorporate "neutral" experts) on Federal and State oversight staff.
- Eliminate or reduce corporate tax breaks or tie them more closely to progress on CSR-type issues.

While a few of these suggestions are more spirited than realistic, all of them deserve a credible public hearing. More to the point: It's important to realize how much unseen power corporations have to control their destiny. The basic intent of this Christmas list of wishes is to take some of that power back if it doesn't start getting used in a more thoughtful, inclusive, and benevolent way.

Facing all change agents are structures, forces, and systems of belief—legal/organizational and psychological/personal—that remain loyal to the idea that the only purpose of business is creating wealth through growth with as few impediments as possible. It's becoming clearer, though, that this narrowly defined mission has outlived its usefulness; the costs, more broadly defined and understood than ever before, are exceeding the benefits.

At the same time, the benefits of the alternatives are becoming just as obvious. This is good news to those of us looking for "proof" that there's more than one way to make a widget. The profit motive behind corporate behavior will never be fully tamed, but if that motive can be tempered with a more open-minded vision of purpose, then the potential of business to heal rather than destroy has a chance of succeeding. The responsibility, once again, falls primarily to the people who run our companies, for it is they who make the key decisions and who will be the architects of that new vision.

CHAPTER 8

Seven Steps to Corporate Transformation

"Meaningful work" is not necessarily work that is exciting and challenging at every moment; it is enough that it be part of a larger endeavor which is infused with meaning.
—WILLIS HARMAN, *Creative Work*

elow I describe seven key areas where companies can begin to reorganize their priorities and more closely align corporate values with personal values. The emphasis is on the software side of business (e.g., vision, purpose, accountability, management) rather than the hardware side (skill development, technical innovation) because therein lie the roots of lasting change. Some of the areas address organizational overhaul—revisioning the primary purpose of a business and the specific outcomes it seeks to achieve. Some address executive/managerial support, such as the important role of leadership in facilitating a shift from one model to another. Nearly all of them ultimately speak to change at an individual/personal level—the power each of us has to revitalize our workplaces by the choices and commitments we make, however modest they might be. Still, no one can change the world by him- or herself; borrowing from a popular idiom, "it takes a community to transform a company." Success will depend on both a belief that change is necessary and the collective will of all to do the work.

1. Values and Purpose

This is where it starts: a clear declaration and understanding of why a company is in business that transcends one-dimensional goals of material conquest. This is basically the heart and soul of any business, the touchstone that people return to when difficult decisions are needed, the "core ideology" that Jim Collins concluded was a key to long-term corporate success. If there is a "noble cause" at the root of an organization's raison d'etre—and there should be—this is where to claim it.

Hallmark Cards, for example, states that "our products and services must enrich people's lives and enhance their relationships," and counts among its values "ethical and moral conduct at all times and in all our relationships." One of Biogen's values is to "tell the truth, even when it appears to be discouraged, and accept nothing less in others." The principle purpose of Eileen Fisher, a clothing store for women, is "to inspire women to be who they are." It is no less dedicated to the needs of its employees. A key corporate value reads, "to nourish well-being through opportunities to learn and grow in mind, body, and spirit." To that end, the company gives every employee two thousand dollars *each year* to use for self-care and personal/spiritual development, with a requirement that they report what they did and how it affected them. Can you imagine working for a company like this?

Lee Hock, founder and former CEO of Visa International and a proponent of a new business model he calls the "chaordic organization"—modeled on the natural workings of the brain—urges companies to clarify the core motivation behind their mission while cautioning them to be careful of what they seek:

> [W]hat is your system of beliefs about how you intend to conduct yourself in pursuit of (your) purpose? If your beliefs are based on the old model of top-down command and control, specialization, special privilege, and nothing but profit, your organization will, in time, turn toxic. . . . If the purpose and principles are con-

structive and healthy, then your organization will take a very different form than anything that you ever imagined.

2. Leadership Commitment

As above, so below: There is little chance that a company will alter its commitments if leadership and management don't believe that changes are necessary. But when it comes to tinkering with such core dictums as "maximizing profits," well, there'd better be an awfully good reason. That's why so few executives embrace, for example, the principles of CSR—their conditioned minds see only loss, not gain, even as evidence supporting the economic wisdom of principled business practice accumulates. A 2002 report conducted by Sustainable Asset Management (SAM), an international investment firm, revealed that only 16 percent of the 1,336 companies surveyed had made specific, proactive commitments to CSR and sustainability. The main reason? CEOs wanted still more proof linking CSR practices to financial and market performance. Such thinking is logical given the normal pressure-packed circumstances under which such decisions are made, but then wouldn't logic also suggest that old ways of doing business are not so bulletproof anymore? A key finding in Ian Mitroff and Elizabeth Denton's seminal work *A Spiritual Audit of Corporate America* was that more and more people want "the ability to realize my full potential as a person" at work, difficult to achieve when their mission and that of their employer is so narrowly defined. Meanwhile, traditional motivational tools are becoming obsolete.

John Dalla Costa believes that nothing short of total "conversion" can change the hearts and minds of corporate decision makers who can't see beyond the status quo. His book *The Ethical Imperative* cites the research of Bernard Lonergan as offering a model of how such a conversion is achieved. "The process is dynamic and continuous," Dalla Costa writes, "but essentially involves four stages. . . . Be attentive.

Be intelligent. Be reasonable. Be responsible." Professor of humanities Paul Woodruff would add at least a fifth: reverence. "Reverence," he writes in his book of that title,

> is the capacity to feel respect in the right way toward the right people, and to feel awe towards an object that transcends particular human interests. When leaders are reverent, they are reverent along with their followers, and their common reverence unites them in feelings that overwhelm personal interests. . . . These feelings take the sting from the tools of leadership—from persuasion, from threats of punishment, from manipulations by means of reward. That is because there are no winners and losers where there is reverence.

Can such human-scale qualities be taught? Yes, if there is a willingness to learn and a belief in the value of the outcomes. They do represent significant challenges for those still mired in traditional roles of power, but the demands of a twenty-first-century workplace require new skills, a larger vision, and, perhaps most importantly, a questioning—and questing—attitude. This may mean convincing skeptical boards of a new environmental policy or standing up to the narrow interests of wealthy shareholders. In other words, goring sacred cows (which, according to the late 1960s activist Abbie Hoffman, "make the best hamburger"). If business is to overcome centuries of conditioning about its role in the world, if leaders truly want to discover the next "new, new thing," one with staying power that will help cement the loyalty of increasingly disenchanted employees without forgoing economic survival, then such breakthrough commitments are needed.

3. Work without Walls

The most powerful tool available for creating an environment of trust and respect in the workplace is complete openness of process. No games, no secrets—just a simple pledge from leadership that what happens in the company is everybody's business, that in fact the only way to meet the challenges of a competitive marketplace is to give every employee full access to information, a chance to participate in decision making, and legitimate channels for constructive feedback, recognition, and dealing with conflict.

Authentic commitments to "work without walls" are built internally into the culture of a company through such tools as open-door policies, open books, and ongoing contact between management and staff, between departments, and peer to peer. Such policy commitments create learning environments where mistakes are treated as opportunities, people are constantly reminded that their jobs and their opinions count, continual training is second nature, and feelings aren't treated as a foreign language. With such encouragement and support, people naturally bring more of themselves to their work. The result: stronger relationships, deeper loyalties, and smarter decisions.

Few organizations will ever achieve total transparency, of course, but many have created remarkably open environments where leaders actually expect employees to become fully engaged in building their company's future. At TDIndustries, a construction and service company, the CEO joins a revolving group of employees for breakfast every couple of weeks to discuss anything that's on their minds. At monthly meetings open to all employees, the company shares sales and forecast information. SAS Institute, which sells "business intelligence" software and services, conducts ongoing employee satisfaction and management feedback surveys; results are circulated and discussed throughout the firm and changes made as appropriate. Its Professional Education and Development Department offers a wide variety of communication and conflict management classes. Far more than exercises in widening information flow—blizzards of meetings, memos, and e-mail on details large and small—these and other "cultures of communication" reflect a deep belief in the inherent wisdom of each individual to do the right thing when trusted to do so and given the right tools.

4. Ethics Policies and Enforcement

Propelled by the scandals that have rocked the business world during the last few years, corporate ethics has evolved from a primarily "legal compliance" issue to a much broader, values-driven component of workplace life that sets standards for how companies treat not only their employees but all affected stakeholder groups. According to Business for Social Responsibility, the most important ethics issues faced by companies today are: conflicts of interest, financial and accounting integrity, corruption and bribery, consumer and employee privacy, truth in advertising, and fair pay. More subtle areas of possible abuse such as harassment, misuse of authority, dishonesty, and so on also raise ethical concerns. These are obviously complicated issues, and even the most eloquent and passionately stated ethics policy won't prevent certain people from doing things they shouldn't, especially when performance standards such as sales goals or share price are at risk.

Nevertheless, a strong policy rigorously enforced puts meat on the bones of a company's statements of values and purpose, and sends a clear message to employees that leadership will not tolerate moral lapses no matter where on the org chart they occur. More and more companies are reaffirming their commitment to ethical conduct through such actions as board oversight, staff training, senior-level advocacy, help lines (phone and digital), whistleblower protections, the hiring of ethics officers, and more. Some have aligned their ethics policies with their core values. Texas Instruments, for example, has reoriented its ethics policy around innovation, integrity, and commitment. It also has developed a bullet-point guideline for helping employees work through ethical dilemmas. Raytheon distributes ethics-awareness booklets and sends all seventy-nine thousand of their worldwide employees through an annual ethics training course.

5. Environmental Responsibility

Despite all the progress that one would think has been made on the environmental front, the planet continues to buckle under the consumptive demands of a growing population—six billion and counting! The WorldWatch Institute, in its State of the World 2002 report, called on the business community to become more actively involved in creating a more sustainable and environmentally sensitive global economy: "The U.N. Environment Programme has struggled to maintain its annual budget of roughly $100 million. At the same time, military expenditures by the world's governments are running at more than $2 billion a day." Perhaps hearing the call, an estimated one thousand business representatives attended the 2002 World Summit on Sustainable Development held in Johannesburg, South Africa; more than one hundred of them were CEOs or Board Chairmen.

And yet countless companies here in the United States, where "green" causes supposedly have made significant gains, are still without an environmental policy or even an efficient recycling program. Few measures of biological health show consistent and reliable improvement. The pressures of a competitive global marketplace and the daily dramas it creates make it all too easy to forego ecological considerations for financial ones, even as evidence accumulates that the two are intertwined. There simply has never been a price tag on the destruction of nature; the value of a devastated wetland, for example, is still treated as a no-cost "externality" of production, and there is great resistance to calculating a "replacement cost." Those who've tried, proponents of a still-obscure discipline called *ecological economics*, invariably conclude that the value of the natural world in its original state outweighs whatever private use it's turned into. Their findings—pitting private gain against public loss—are more often ignored than debated, and the public usually suffers.

Undeterred, a persistent and growing chorus of activists, from schoolchildren and consumer groups to religious organizations and business leaders themselves, are telling the corporate world that a healthy environment is more important than ever, and companies are slowly responding. Some, such as computer maker NEC, have integrated an ecological ethic into every level of its manufacturing process. Norm Thompson Outfitters has a Sustainability Toolkit and Scorecard for helping its buyers evaluate the environmental integrity of source materials for its clothing lines. Interface chairman Ray Anderson decided to redesign his carpet manufacturing firm's entire production process after reading Paul Hawken's *The Ecology of Commerce*. Xerox, General Motors, and Verifone (a subsidiary of Hewlett-Packard) have documented millions of dollars saved by instituting stricter environmental controls on their business operations. Others have launched internal audits and assigned management teams to come up with enlightened policies and plans. International standards and principles have been developed to give companies benchmark goals while encouraging them to file reports on their progress. There is no shortage of actions to take and resources available for businesses that are truly serious about lessening their impact on planet Earth.

6. Social Responsibility

Visionary companies in the twenty-first century will also make their mark by how they interact with the communities they affect, both those in which they operate directly and those in other countries that provide raw materials or production facilities. Such businesses will proactively develop programs and policies that respect the interests of these local communities. This is especially important in the developing world, which suffers a history of Western economic exploitation, but even here in the United States there is much that companies can do to become better citizens in ways that aren't measured solely by the jobs they create or the taxes they pay. I'm not talking about underwriting a new baseball stadium that ends up bearing a corporate logo on its marquee, but rather participating at a very human level in boosting the livability and communal strength of a place.

Some philanthropic ventures have strategic elements that are consistent with a company's values and mission, such as State Farm Insurance's low-income community revitalization program. In others, resources are offered freely, without expectation of specific returns. No matter the approach, such efforts can take many forms, everything from fund raising and charity sponsorships to donations of executive expertise. Some companies engage their employees with paid volunteer time and positions on advisory committees. A genuine spirit of benevolence and buy-in can only improve a company's profile, not just within its community but also among its employees.

On a global level, recognition is growing that it's not okay to treat local workers with any less respect than those employed at home. Marjorie Kelly raises issues of fair profit, maximum profit, and economic justice when she asserts, "If a company can get away with paying twenty cents an hour it will, even if paying forty cents doesn't hurt it." Such practices are being scrutinized; Nike and others, for example, have been slammed for ignoring inadequate working conditions and using unfair labor practices to manufacture products in developing countries. (To Nike's credit, it participated, along with a handful of other companies, in the Fair Labor Association's first-ever external monitoring of labor practices in non-U.S. supplier manufacturing plants, carried out from August 1, 2001, through July 31, 2002. An improved record removed some of the tarnish off Nike's reputation, but the FLA report still flagged incidents of noncompliance among the seven companies profiled. Meanwhile, numerous other multinationals continue to exploit local workers as they outsource more jobs and take advantage of developing countries' economic vulnerability.)

Whether responding to criticism or following their own corporate conscience, growing numbers of companies are embracing social responsibility. In the coffee industry, enlightened firms are aligning themselves with networks of "fair-trade" businesses, which attempt to ensure that those who create the goods—in this case coffee growers—are paid a fair or living wage for their efforts. Cisco has partnered with the United Nations Development Program (UNDP) to launch NetAid, which "aims to mobilize support for an end to extreme poverty by bringing individuals, companies and organizations together in ways that expand opportunities for the world's poorest families and communities." Chiquita Brands International, a former poster child for companies doing bad things overseas, has become a leader on many fronts; it adheres to the Rainforest Alliance's Better Banana Project standard, which calls for reducing the use of toxic chemicals, and was given a solid human rights scorecard by independent auditors in 2003 for its operations in Columbia, Costa Rica, and Panama. These companies and others prove once again that there are lots of intelligent ways to put people and the planet in front of profit and still be financially viable.

7. Accountability/Transparency

The real test of a company's commitment to responsible business practice is its willingness to develop or accept existing standards for activities beyond the strictly financial, monitor progress in meeting those standards, and then announce the results to stakeholder groups in its annual report or a format specifically designed to present such information. Achieving measurable results in such a broad range of areas is a tall order for any company, but once such commitments are made, the momentum to keep reaching builds, engaging the workforce in ways that may not have been possible when a company's mission was less noble.

Such transparency is a courageous act; reporting standards are hardly uniform, the interrelationship of issues is complex, and disclosure opens up a company to criticism from a variety of interest groups eager to test reality against ideals. But standards do exist, technical as well as moral, and the number of companies stepping forward to make their inner workings visible to the rest of the world—or at least to their own employees—is growing. According to BSR, "It is estimated that 500 companies now issue comprehensive reports on their social and environmental activities and impacts, a dramatic increase over the seven reports that were issued in 1990, while thousands of companies produce reports on aspects of CSR performance like the environment or philanthropy." Such reporting is still voluntary as opposed to mandatory, but growing demands from stakeholder groups for across-the-board details on corporate performance is keeping the pressure up.

Again I wonder: with so many examples of real companies doing good works and reaping both quantitative and qualitative rewards, why aren't more of them doing it? What prevents people in power from making decisions that they know in their hearts are ethically, socially, and ecologically superior to those that they so often make? Well, as we have seen, this question isn't simple, and neither is the answer.

At an organizational level, transforming a company from the ground up takes an enormous amount of passion, focus, and patience, qualities that aren't always in ready supply. Even small movements in a conscious direction can be difficult to navigate through existing webs of political and economic stickiness. Competitive pressures, career ambitions, "old boy" networks, and so on are some of the obstacles to playing by different rules. Another problem with most change efforts is that they don't usually happen in a vacuum. In order for one thing to change and/or stay changed, other things must change as well. Advocates of prison recovery, for instance, recognize that it's one thing to equip the incarcerated with life management skills while they're in prison, and quite another to control their environment—family situations, peer pressures, job shortages, racial biases—when they get out. In the workplace, it helps considerably when executive management takes a leadership position in pushing corporate boundaries, but staying on course requires company-wide buy-in, systems of accountability, communication, training, ingenuity, and persistence, especially when the results aren't immediately apparent. Finally there is the nagging challenge of outfoxing the oppressive creed of maximizing profit and shareholder wealth, the dominant driver of most business activity.

Fortunately, more and more leaders and their companies are coming to believe in the wisdom of another way. Those who take up the cause will discover multiple avenues for expressing a larger vision of service and corporate citizenship, thereby transforming their workplaces, igniting the enthusiasm of those who work in them, and healing some of the wounds that business-as-usual has made in its narrow-minded pursuits. As this chapter has suggested, there are many places to launch such a commitment. The challenge is breaking free from the institutional and psychological constraints that keep us bound to old ways of running a business. How can business leaders disengage from the tyranny of corporate culture and the bottom line and begin to think independently, intentionally, and compassionately? How do we integrate the practical and the visionary in the face of legitimate survival fears and the pressure to conform? How can we elevate both personal and corporate values to a new and higher level of alignment? These are central considerations if workplace transformation and long-term sustainability are the objectives.

PART 4

The Practice: A Path for Individuals

CHAPTER 9

Reclaiming Our Authentic Self

When we are no longer able to change a situation . . . we are challenged to change ourselves.
—Victor Frankl, Holocaust survivor, writer, psychoanalyst

In her groundbreaking 1987 book *Do What You Love, the Money Will Follow*, Marsha Sinetar invited readers to live out their desire of creating work that resonated from their deepest selves. She invoked the dreams we may have had as children, the natural talents we organically felt drawn to express but which were stifled by no-nonsense parents who feared for our future. "You want to be a painter, a musician, a ballet dancer? Just do your homework." I wanted to be a professional bowler!

Discussing the true nature of vocation and how it has been distorted over time, educator Parker Palmer writes in *Yes! A Journal of Positive Futures*:

> We arrive in this world with birthright gifts—then we spend the first half of our lives abandoning them or letting others disabuse us of them. As young people, we are surrounded by expectations that may have little to do with who we really are, expectations held by people who are not trying to discern our selfhood but to fit us into slots. In families, schools, workplaces, and religious

communities, we are trained away from true self toward images of acceptability; under social pressures like racism and sexism our original shape is deformed beyond recognition; and we ourselves, driven by fear, too often betray true self to gain the approval of others.

Sinetar and Palmer speak to the part of us that feels suppressed by the past and by the conditions of our employment, that still has hopes of finding better, more meaningful work or finding that meaning in the work we already do.

This book has spent much time discussing *why* our work doesn't satisfy us. Workplace culture, the American work ethic, and society's addiction to materialism have a tremendous impact on the role that work has in our lives. Their influence is structural and deep. Powerful forces without moral or ethical grounding have largely controlled the evolution of business and work and our place in them. There is often no greater meaning attached to what we buy or sell or serve than how much money it will make or save us or how much comfort it will provide. Selling life insurance, for example, is probably for most sales-people not so much about ensuring that the impact of an unexpected tragedy will be lessened on a grieving family but that a commission is made on the transaction. Again, in a money-driven world some of this thinking is natural, but materialism and narrow self-interest have come to dominate our priorities. The result: an efficient system of need fulfillment on a largely superficial level.

Is this who we really are? Is this what we really want? Just as we have adapted to our present circumstances, so too can we shift gears and reorient ourselves toward a more sustainable and life-giving reality. Connecting with a deeper source of inspiration requires that we acknowledge the impact that these influences have had on the choices we've made, and then start making new decisions based on a larger understanding of who we are at work, who we want to become, and what is really most important to us. This is where the meaning that has been so elusive in our jobs will make itself known to us.

Negative Conditioning or Human Nature?

I have a hypothesis, and it runs something like this: The only way to regain some control over our workplace experience and reshape it in a more meaningful way is to separate our identity from that of the company we work for, disengage from the expectations that society has for us, and decide anew the kind of relationship we want with our jobs. To do this we need to take a close look at our basic attitudes toward work (such as clarifying our purpose, discussed in chapter 2) and at the same time create a stronger link between the values that we strive to live by and the potential of work for helping us do that.

Needless to say, this is easier said than done, for rarely do we act with such a heightened sense of intent and self-awareness. We are highly influenced by the social and economic rules of society and workplace culture and by the coping strategies we developed while growing up. Most specialists in personality profiling will tell you that many of the characteristics and behaviors that define who we are were hardwired in childhood. The overachiever, the underachiever, the rebel, the jock, the nerd—such conditioned psychological and emotional responses became our primary identities. Sometimes we're aware of them in a "There I go again" kind of way—screaming at a coworker or capitulating to an unjust supervisor or even withdrawing from a true gesture of friendship. More likely we don't give our behaviors a second thought, continuing to relate to our world from a seemingly fixed template of mistrust, need, and self-preservation. Desperate for acknowledgment, pinned in by hierarchy, fearful that we'll be labeled Cs instead of Bs, we sometimes allow ourselves to take the lower road or stand mute on the sidelines watching others succumb to lesser motives.

Someone I know in the hospitality industry recounts tale after tale of managers eavesdropping behind doors or tapping into phone calls or taking credit for someone else's work or treating subordinates like children. Rick, a high-tech customer service rep, was disheartened by a lack of justice in his department:

> Some agents would simply hang up on people in order to make it look like they were making more calls. I would spend five minutes working with a customer because they needed it but on paper it looks like I'm a slackard, that my "churn" was low. Sometimes those other people would get caught and fired but most of the time they got away with it because it's such a big company that nobody notices or management doesn't care. You could be doing the best job in the department but because someone didn't like you, you didn't get the same raises or opportunities. The politics of it all was so hard on me I had to get out.

A *Seattle Times* article in a local newspaper brought up an interesting point when it noted that the well-publicized antics of Wall Street didn't seem all that different from those of any decent-sized company.

> Bosses who cover their backsides? Our executive suites are stuffed with them. Toadies who twist the facts to get promotions? That sounds like the guy at the next desk. Backstabbing colleagues? It isn't safe to walk these corridors. Feuding between departments? Don't get us started on that mob in sales. Open contempt for the customer? Ahem, no. We love our customers.

Discussing in the same article civil fraud charges filed by the Massachusetts Secretary of State against Credit Suisse First Boston and some of the damning e-mail correspondence uncovered in the investigation, the author concluded, "The suspicion must be that, in part at least, what [the state is] prosecuting is human nature. If every dysfunctional office is going to be prosecuted, they are going to need some very big jails."

Look at your own place of work and objectively consider your behavior and that of your colleagues. Why do people do what they do? What role do I play, what values do I bring—or leave out? Is "human nature" at the root of workplace dysfunction or do we have more control over our impulses than we think?

I believe that human nature does play a role in the way that it has been damaged by trauma or torqued by the chaos and insensitivity of modern life; we have formed our defenses and carry them into our jobs. At the same time, we are also the products of our training—family, education, and culture have conditioned us to perceive and respond to our environment in certain ways. Not surprisingly, the yearning for a deeper experience of work—an impulse that originates from outside that training—sets up a conflict with this "conditioned self," the one enmeshed in the values of a system built on fear, status, and acquisition. The result: a tug of war between what we want to experience and the patterns of coping we've grown used to. In short, it feels easier to play by old rules than new ones. This is where the battle will ultimately be won or lost—within our own psyches as we confront powerful forces of compromise and limitation that we have internalized over the years. To apply a higher purpose to the work we do and the companies we work for, we must go inside ourselves and find it.

The Power of Self-Awareness

I am not a psychologist so I need to tread cautiously here, but I suspect that the solution to many of our problems lies in (1) greater self-knowledge and (2) exploring the gap between who we intuitively know ourselves to be, defined by our most idealistic values and goals, and the decisions we actually make in the world. As David Whyte wrote in *Crossing the Unknown Sea*, "People must be encouraged not only to know their craft, their products, their work and the people they serve, but to know a little of themselves."

"Knowing oneself," to the extent we have pursued it at all, is something that all spiritual traditions will tell you is a lifelong quest. The typical "self" has many layers, from the outermost surface/social self that we present to the world around us, to the deepest experience of the self that usually lies buried or veiled or distorted by the levels above. This surface, or "functional," self is made up of unconscious or barely conscious patterns of thinking and feeling that have cemented over time and now operate most of the controls of our psyche. It affects every choice we make and every interaction we have. And yet despite its constant influence we're usually ignorant of how it operates or what it wants. We are going with the flow, swept up in the dramas of our lives with little time for careful reflection and reaction. If we did make such time for ourselves, we would start to notice that how we act in the world does not always reflect how we think we should have acted. Why *did* I lose my temper at the meeting this morning?

I believe that much of what happens at work, from a personal to an organizational level, is the end result of a complicated process that begins internally with each individual's self-concept, motivations, fears, and desires. If our experience at work is unpleasant or worse, how are we contributing to that? What is going on inside of us that makes an experience this way or that? What can we do to influence the outcome not just of our time at work but the mission of the company we work for? Where do we find the will to make positive contributions, even if those around us are playing by different rules? These are some of the questions we must ask—and answer—if we are to get back in touch with a deeper sense of personal purpose that is bigger than our circumstances, bigger than the notions we have come to believe about work and its potential.

Cultivating self-awareness—becoming familiar with your own patterns of behavior and emotional character—is a critical first step in this reconditioning process. It's when you start waking up to who you are at work. Author Daniel Goleman identifies self-awareness as one of the four major components of what he calls "emotional intelligence." Most of us usually react to our work environment from the conditioned or coping self discussed above. We are basically in survival mode, content to get through a day without any serious damage and without taking any risks. The search for meaning, however, inevitably brings us closer to what is really going on. That's when we start to discover how little of ourselves we've brought to our jobs and how painful it is to realize that. Inspired by the words of poet/philosopher John O'Donohue, Cheryl Peppers and Alan Briskin write in *Bringing Your Soul to Work*, "When there becomes too great a discrepancy between the life we lead and the worlds that collide in our heart, we can experience life and work as flat and dull." Or worse.

The power of self-awareness is in revealing ourselves to ourselves, as honestly as we can, perhaps for the first time. In *The Art of Happiness at Work*, the Dalai Lama, in a series of conversations with psychiatrist Howard Cutler, suggests that one of the keys to workplace satisfaction is developing "a sense of self that is grounded in reality, an undistorted recognition of one's abilities and characteristics." He's asking that we simply acknowledge what we see without judgment, both our strengths and weaknesses, and take responsibility for our attitudes and behaviors. Tools such as personality tests can help—Are you an ISTP, an ESFP, a Pleaser, a Striver, a Critical Judge?—and more and more companies are relying on them to build teams and safe-proof their hiring process. But the reality is that each individual persona is a moving target and situation specific; we are dynamic, subjective, and made up of multiple inner voices, each one with its own agenda. In short, we are complicated beings. "At most," wrote one reporter summarizing the state of personality research, "we can say personality is based on an individual's most consistent internal responses to life experiences, and that a self-aware person is aware of these responses."

It's been said that there are three areas of knowledge:

1. What you know.
2. What you know you don't know but know where to find out.
3. What you don't know you don't know.

The third one is by far the largest of the three, and certainly the scariest. It is the dark well of discovery and disclosure that reveals itself when we least expect it, often when we are problem solving or taking risks. It reminds us that our perspective of a situation is not necessarily the largest or truest reality of it. Everyone involved in a problem or a disagreement or an exchange of views has a piece of the truth to contribute. Our responsibility is to consider all interactions as opportunities for self-discovery and truth seeking.

Self-awareness is the key to this third category of knowledge. It begins to reveal how our minds work, where our fears and desires reside. It brings us closer to knowing whether our outside behavior is consistent with what we feel inside and, more importantly, whether that behavior reflects the values we want to live by. It helps us to see where in our work we get blocked as we seek to bring a higher quality of spirit and skill to our trade. In moments of frustration we can slow things down and catch ourselves before an overreactive mind says something that later we wish it hadn't. Self-aware people will often think twice before responding to a situation, taking a moment to discern what lies beneath an initial response. How we interpret a situation makes all the difference in how we react. Something as simple as perpetuating an unflattering rumor about a new manager will raise a red flag to those who may have gone along with it in the past but now realize that this isn't the kind of person they aspire to be.

Over time, the self-aware person will begin to develop a maturity and a personal ethic that is immune from outside influences, guiding their behavior and keeping them grounded no matter the circumstance. "When you are unconscious," writes Let Davidson in *Wisdom at Work*, you remain a mechanical victim of your own subliminal mental tendencies, painful habits, and counterproductive patterns. Heightened self-awareness reveals these habits and patterns, so that you can deal with them. You can accept them, let them go, or change them. Awareness gives you the choice to respond appropriately, to channel your power in the directions you choose.

Such a practice is especially valuable when we interact with others, a frequent source of head-banging frustration. Increasing our capacity to communicate from an aware, unprogrammed place, free from emotional conditioning and its many triggers, will have an enormous impact on our ability both to protect ourselves from and build relationships with those we work with.

The practice of self-awareness is a valuable ally in determining our purpose both in and out of work—what we want to accomplish personally and professionally. Those driven by financial motivations, for example, would assess their behavior based on whether it serves that particular purpose. Others with strong moral or ethical beliefs would likewise match their behavior with those values. Needless to say, it's important to clarify just what values are closest to our heart. The extent to which those values are felt in our personal and professional lives is the extent to which we are living from our core beliefs. If the point of a meaningful work life is to connect it with the larger purposes we have for ourselves and for how we'd like the world to be, then self-awareness and value clarity will tell us whether or not our actions are bringing us closer to those goals.

In thinking about these ideas I was struck by the following quote from an *Atlantic Monthly* article, which really gave me hope: "The thrust for a moral and ethical structure that claims spiritual roots, the need to believe in an order greater than this earthly one, is stronger than ever." This statement was not directed specifically to the work-place but it could have been. And spirituality, not in a religious sense but in the sense of something that connects us at a human level, is an imperative that supercedes dogma and policies and goes right to the heart.

Indeed, past conditioning can only be undone when we allow ourselves to get closer to the things that make us feel as if we are really making a difference in the world. "Our deepest calling is to grow into our own authentic selfhood," writes Parker Palmer in his *Yes!* article, "whether or not it conforms to some image of who we ought to be. As we do so, we will not only find the joy that every human being seeks—we will also find our path of authentic service in the world. True vocation joins self and service."

In many of our workplaces, such a confluence seems impossible to achieve. Where is the global ethic in retail sales? What does software design have to do with self-realization? How can I "be myself" when all this other stuff is going on? These are legitimate questions, and yet even in the midst of our confusion, under all the layers of conditioning we have endured, there will be a thread of authenticity that connects us to a deeper knowledge of ourselves and our longing to experience a sane and healthy work life. And it may be less a matter of finding what Palmer calls "true vocation" than of using the work we do—no matter what it is—to grow emotionally, psychologically, and even spiritually.

CHAPTER 10

Work from the Inside Out

*Artful work requires the consistent and conscious use of the self.
As the artist creates the work, the work creates the artist. . . . The
materials of the moment are more than the physical things in
front of us—more than simply the clay, a report from a task
force, a page of numbers, a set of charts, a machine, or ideas
written on a white board. The materials of the moment include
emotion and spirit. When we include them, we become who we
truly are and bring all of ourselves to our work. We become cen-
tered and artful.*
—DICK RICHARDS, *Artful Work*

Barbara Waugh, author of *The Soul in the Computer* and for
twenty years (and counting) an executive with Hewlett-Packard,
has made a career out of stirring things up. From her early
years as a women's rights activist to her current position as "change
agent" at H-P, she has made it her mission to remake the technology
giant—or at least certain parts of it—using communication, collaboration, and creativity to help people work together to make positive
things happen. I bring her up at the beginning of this chapter because
she, as much as anyone, has been doing the difficult work of real workplace transformation, and from her years of experience in the trenches
has gained some legitimate insights into how such changes occur. She,
along with a colleague, Kristin Cobble, summarized them in a booklet

called "The Self-Organizing Transformation of Hewlett-Packard Laboratories." A few of the more relevant are the following:

1. Think small. "Help happen what wants to happen. Assume resistance is a valid response and don't try to change it. Over a short time, small-scale short-term efforts, fueled by the passion of the people leading them, result in large-scale long-range transformation."

2. Focus on the task at hand. "As human beings, when we're gathered together to do something and we don't know what it is, we don't know how to tell if we're doing it or not, and we are going to go crazy. Set your charter to do things that can actually be accomplished with the people you have, with the resources at hand. That doesn't mean you have to dream small. But dreams are the context for your task, not the task itself."

3. Be the change you wish to see. "If we want to see more risk-taking, we must ourselves take more risks. If we want people to dream bigger dreams, we must ourselves dream bigger dreams. If we want the whole person to come to work, we must bring all of ourselves to work."

Applying her observations on transformation to a personal level, Waugh seems to be saying that the ultimate responsibility for change is ours and that change happens when people take small steps toward specific, achievable goals rather than expect others to do it for them. Pretty basic advice—common sense, really—but the *impetus* to change and taking the steps required can be difficult to sustain in the drama-filled environments that characterize much of our personal and work life.

The suggestions in this chapter are not about helping one navigate the labyrinth of office politics or revitalize a career path, however useful such ends are. And they may not be strong enough to overcome entrenched power dynamics or structurally unjust workplaces. But they can make a positive difference no matter the situation. They are designed to help establish a stronger sense of inner direction and personal presence from which to act, react, and choose with more control and self-awareness. As we stay focused on the present moment, manage our feelings more effectively, and overcome the auto-response mechanism of the conditioned self, we start making wiser decisions and relating to our environment in a fresh, authentic way that is unique to who we are and true to our highest values. We start becoming ourselves at work. Over time, meaning will emerge not because our job or our employer has changed but because we have.

Six Tools for Remaking Our Work

When we learn to manage the boundaries between our work life and our private life and start putting more of ourselves into them both, then the lines begin to blur between who we are and what we do. It becomes more difficult to compartmentalize our experiences, to put work in one box and family in another and play in yet a third. This doesn't mean that we have to drag our jobs home or to the beach or to wherever we are when we aren't at work. It does mean that we have the opportunity to create an emotional and psychological seamlessness to how we experience and respond to the events and challenges of our day, engaging as much of our whole selves—not just our head or hands but also our heart, vision, spirit, creativity, and passion—as we are able to do.

In its most "advanced" form, this seamlessness takes on the qualities of *flow*, which psychologist Mihaly Csikszentmihalyi has defined as "the holistic sensation that people feel with total involvement," not dissimilar to Martin Seligman's description of one of the three paths to happiness. And yet such seamlessness does not necessarily lead to happiness, nor does "meaningful" work. In fact, when our experience of work deepens, it matters less whether or not we are happy—though we may very well be—because it's the process that counts. At the same time, the satisfaction we end up experiencing is more than just happiness; it can approach fulfillment. Importantly, the quest for Csikszentmihalyi's groove can only be advanced incrementally, in small steps. More to the point, it is a byproduct of the efforts that precede it, not so much a cognized goal. I favor means over ends because we live in the present, not the future; deal wisely with the present and the future usually takes care of itself.

Most of the workplaces I'm familiar with are pretty hectic scenes, everyone tanked up on coffee and adrenaline and deal-making and deadlines. The value of the present is measured by how close it is getting you to the future. The tools presented below thus may seem naive in the face of such intoxicating intensity. They require thought, commitment, patience, and time, and a bit of slowing down, because meaning and wisdom—and certainly peace of mind—are rarely found in the express lane. Some of the tools have a decidedly Eastern flavor. Such philosophies have long emphasized the development of inner skills for living life more wisely, and seeking meaning in today's workplaces, where decisions are complex and every situation unique, qualifies for such dexterity.

1. Start from Where You Are

For some of us, the job itself is an obstacle to deeper satisfaction when we perceive it as less than what we think we are capable of doing. I certainly had that experience in the casino once I'd been there a few years, and in a few other jobs as well. "I'm a dice dealer, for crissakes! Where's the nobility in that?" Have you ever been asked "So, what do you do?" and felt a quiver of shame—or a surge of ego—inside? In a world that judges people by what they do, we've become overly sensitized to what our work says about who we are. The impacts of such judgments affect our sense of self-worth, which seems to have less to do with the actual self than with how others regard and respect that self. Even apparently successful corporate executives can struggle with feelings of inferiority and failure.

Vulnerable to the whims and wrong-mindedness of a value-dysfunctional world, it's thus no wonder that our self-esteem is greatly influenced by how we perceive our work and how others perceive it. James M. Childs Jr., in his book *Ethics in Business: Faith at Work*, talks about the difference between a "nobody" and a "somebody":

> In our work life we are especially prone to linking self-worth to generally accepted indicators of success. If we are doing well on the job and getting recognized for it or we have jobs that seem meaningful and important, we are thereby endowed with a sense of being "somebody." When we experience the opposite, we fear that we are "nobodies." The nature of our occupations and the success we have in them are enormously powerful factors in our own sense of identity and well-being.

Nevertheless, a meaningful work life is not job specific. I have seen as much if not more dignity and grace and joy in a parking lot attendant than in many well-tailored executives. True, they don't have the same responsibilities: parking cars cannot be compared to sweating over multimillion-dollar mergers. But at the core all work is relative, and our experience of it will largely depend on what we bring to it. Every job has value and every job takes skill.

Think of your own workplace. Take a single day, or even a single hour, and go through it minute by minute. Make a list of everything you do, from the simplest task to the most challenging, and all the ways you connect with others. Leave nothing out. Looking this closely at your job, you may be surprised at everything it takes to do it well. What we think are an endless number of busy hours leading to an exhausting conclusion is in fact a series of chances for being a decent person and doing honorable work. This is where purpose comes in. Are our actions meeting the needs of others in just a functional way—

accurately revising a contract or submitting a report on time—or do they reflect a broader awareness and intention? Purpose with a small *p*—doing our work well, even going that extra step—follows from Purpose with a capital *P*, the commitment to use one's work as a means of becoming a better human.

Martin Luther King, Jr., once said "If you are called to be a streetsweeper, you should sweep streets even as Michelangelo painted, or Beethoven composed music, or Shakespeare wrote poetry." The late Canadian politician and literary figure Lord Tweedsmuir wrote, "I would be content with any job, however thankless, in any quarter, however remote, if I had a chance of making a corner of the desert blossom and a solitary place glad." As these two great statesmen imply, the work we do is no better or worse than the quality of the person we put into it. This doesn't mean that we can't aspire to greater things or acknowledge the limitations of our current jobs; improving our self or our situation or our skills is a natural and healthy instinct. It suggests instead that the work we do, no matter what kind, is not the measure of who we are; what counts is how we do that work. In a seemingly senseless, uncaring, and faceless world, we find meaning where we can, no less so a cab driver than a CEO; in a handshake, a smile, a simple act of kindness.

2. Apply Beginner's Mind

In his classic book *Zen Mind, Beginner's Mind*, Shunryu Suzuki-roshi talks about the importance of being open and curious, unattached to results or goals. The danger in being an expert, he warns, is that the field of possibilities is limited since the mind is already crammed with answers. In a beginner's mind, however, everything is an adventure, a *learning*. An open mind can hold much more than a closed one. It's more versatile and responsive, bending but never breaking. In her 1996 Nobel Prize lecture, "The Poet and the World," Polish poet Wislawa Szymborska wrote about the danger of being an expert:

[K]nowledge that doesn't lead to new questions quickly dies out; it fails to maintain the temperature required for sustaining life .... This is why I value that little phrase "I don't know" so highly. It's small, but it flies on mighty wings. It expands our lives to include spaces within us as well as the outer expanses in which our tiny Earth hangs suspended.

One of the obstacles to overcoming disenchantment with work is that we assume we've seen and tried it all, that we know the score and there's nothing else we can do. Cynicism and despair replace hope and investigation. By comparison, the spirit of beginner's mind sees every moment, or at least most of them, as full of revelation. What is new here, what don't I know? Have you ever had the experience of seeing something for the first time that in fact you have seen countless times before, such as a farmhouse along a well-traveled road or the garden in your backyard? When it happens the freshness is startling, close to an altered state. This is the routine-shattering potential of seeing our workplaces with fresh eyes.

And so part of making work meaningful is using it to study both ourselves and others—psychologically, emotionally, ethically. In this way we bring the meaning to our work if it doesn't readily offer it to us. In the process, we begin to learn things that might help us. Think of yourself as an anthropologist and your workplace as the target culture. Your mission is to understand what's going on. On one level it may seem obvious—for example, ambitious managers making bad decisions to protect their insecurities. Dip below the surface, though, and other realities will reveal themselves, from subtle office politics and alliances to complicated personal feelings that may be masked by easy-going attitudes. Trained both on the world around you and the one inside you, such openness to larger truths can lead to surprising insights and unexpected successes.

Some years ago, Timothy Gallwey, author of *The Inner Game of Tennis* and other similarly titled books, was brought in by AT&T to help make their operators' job "less threatening and more interesting." This oft-maligned group labors under ceaseless pressure while fighting boredom, repetition, and lots of disgruntled callers. It was estimated that each operator handles about seven hundred calls a day, one right after the other, with little or no time to prepare for the next question or complaint or to recover from the previous one. Gallwey's game plan was to help them control their experiences by teaching them to pay closer attention to each caller, identifying the caller's mood and imagining what they might look like. Essentially, he was asking them to humanize the people at the other end of the line while protecting their own vulnerability. He suggested that they use an awareness technique of evaluating those voices moment by moment and then assigning a number to the intensity of the emotion they were hearing, such as Angry 4, Angry 8, and so on. This detachment produced some surprising results:

1. They "changed the game" by adding a task that wasn't directly related to the business at hand. As a result, they altered potentially disruptive exchanges by perceiving a caller's anger not as a personal attack but as something simply to be aware of. In so doing, they were able to keep their own emotions out of it and resolve the issue more effectively.
2. By keeping their cool, they helped to defuse the caller's frustration level.
3. By humanizing the experience and adding the element of control, boredom and stress levels were reduced and the job became more interesting.

When learning becomes a primary objective and beginner's mind the tool to pursue it, life takes on the quality of a university and your job one of the classrooms. It "changes the game" and gives you some control. Now, sometimes this will be impossible. We have multiple triggers and deep-rooted patterns that gladly spring into action when provoked. If someone starts trashing a report that I've spent weeks putting together, it will be difficult to go into Zen-like acceptance about it. I'm invested in the work, my ego is engaged, I may be trying to impress a boss, and the source of the criticism may be less than a friend. But if I can find the strength to respond from a more open part of me than punch-in-the-nose reactionary, I may learn something important while defending my position with more grace.

3. The Power of Mindfulness

Central to the pursuit of "conscious" work is the practice of mindfulness. Similar to self-awareness but more outwardly focused, mindfulness is the energy that helps one to "be here now" and approach one's work as something more than a tedious obligation. In such an attentive state we make meaningful contact with our workplace surroundings: the stress—or joy—in a coworker's voice, the "feeling tone" of a meeting, the integrity of a potential business client. A perceptive waitress may observe subtle discontent coming from the new cook or the loneliness of the guy sipping coffee at the far table. A school bus driver might notice the boy with the sad eyes or the girl with the tattered skirt. Think about a recent workday and try to recall some of the impressions you had about your interactions with the people there. Does anything or anyone stand out: your boss, a coworker, a customer? Was there a particular conversation or exchange that could have been handled differently or that took you by surprise? How did you respond, and how could you have responded? Did you learn anything new about the politics or the people involved? If yes, does knowing these things make that day a little more interesting or meaningful for you?

Reviewing the day in this way can start to sensitize our antennae until mindfulness grows into an active part of the work self. It's a matter of training oneself to be alert and responsive. The complexity of the world around you deepens as new information starts flowing in; you feel more connected and involved. Learning to identify the psycho/emotional, below-the-surface realities that may underlie someone's behavior helps us make more thoughtful decisions about how and when to respond, or even if a response is called for. Over time, the practice of mindfulness can turn what might otherwise be just another ho-hum irritation into an opportunity for knowledge and compassionate response. Being this aware takes us out of our isolation and into direct relationship. It's one of the tools that can make a workplace more than just a job.

"Perhaps it would be just in a daily lifelong attitude of 'seeing' that the noisy, chaotic activity I call my job could become a support for my attention instead of a distraction," wrote essayist Jean Kinkead Martine about her position in an advertising agency. "Perhaps, if I attend to the reality that is in front of me moment by moment—phone, pencil, boss, coffee—constantly failing, accepting to fail and to begin again—this perfectly ordinary work I do might become extraordinary work, might even become my craft."

Not every detail is worthy of such attention, of course, but as we exercise the skill of mindfulness and it becomes second nature—always "on"—we develop skills of discernment, helping us to determine the relative importance of things and what we can and cannot control. We will also start accessing our intuition, for as we quiet ourselves enough to observe, we open the door to other sources of knowing.

I recall a friend of mine telling me of a conversation she had one afternoon with an overworked conference planner. Lynn had called this person to verify a previous arrangement; the planner had been besieged by similar calls all morning and saw Lynn as just another irritating interruption. Lynn, noting the tension in this woman's voice and responding thoughtfully rather than reactively, said something like "It sounds like you're having a bad day." The planner immediately softened. "You wouldn't believe it." Rather than a confrontation of attitudes, the two shared a pleasant few minutes together and each went away feeling a little better. This was one of those small but unexpected moments of real contact that can make a tangible difference in our work lives. As Thich Nhat Hanh reminds us, "When the phone rings, take three deep breaths before answering it. You may never talk to that person again."

When we start acknowledging the needs of others, we illuminate our own emotions and thoughts as we carry out the tasks of our work. "Denise seems unsure of herself. I could take over the project and score some points with the boss, or bring her back in and share the rewards." Noticing a colleague's unease and how we choose to respond is where mindfulness and self-awareness meet. In the process of interacting with others and paying attention to what is happening, we begin to work out our own stuff *right there, right in the moment.* As in any intimate relationship where this level of commitment is made, our work life becomes another mirror for who we are, and yet another source of meaning is revealed.

4. The Tao of Service

In Hermann Hesse's novel *The Journey to the East,* an assortment of fictional figures—Don Quixote, Siddhartha, Demian, and others—are on a collective pilgrimage of spiritual purpose as members of what Hesse calls The League. Among them is a man named Leo the Server, whom Hesse describes as one of the party's servants:

> He helped to carry the luggage and was often assigned to the personal service of the Speaker. This unaffected man had something so pleasing, so unobtrusively winning about him, that everyone loved him. He did his work gaily, usually sang or whistled as he went along, was never seen except when needed—in fact, an ideal servant.

Despite the obvious capabilities of the group's members, however, they fall into disarray when Leo inexplicably disappears several months into the journey. "On that cool autumn morning when it was discovered that our servant Leo was missing and that all search for him remained fruitless," recalls one of Hesse's characters, "I was certainly not the only one who, for the first time, had a feeling of impending disaster and menacing destiny." And later: "Hardly had Leo left us when faith and concord amongst us was at an end; it was as if the life-blood of our group flowed away from an invisible wound." Indeed, the group never recovers, and many if its members wander off in confusion and despair, the pilgrimage abandoned.

The story conveys the sometimes imperceptible yet essential contribution made by the "servers" among us, whose selfless efforts are the invisible glue that often keeps the whole from coming undone. Not coincidently, Leo turned out to be the leader of The League, who in serving those near him honored his larger commitment to a higher purpose. For he knew that to serve is the key to contentment, and that to place the needs of one's ego above those of the greater community is to bow to a lesser god.

When *giving* becomes one of the central motivations in our work, we are honoring those around us and embracing them as fellow travelers. Being of service is not about giving up your power but empowering yourself to make a positive difference in the world. Joyfully contributing to someone else's life—even in a small way—feeds our own sense of personal meaning. James Childs writes in *Ethics in Business* that Jesus' teachings on service were revolutionary.

> For the Greeks, ruling was the truly fulfilling position to which one should aspire, not serving. Serving was considered undesirable and undignified. The service of the statesman to the state was honorable, but it was still thought of as self-fulfilling rather than an exercise in self-giving. For Jesus, service and servanthood are the marks of true discipleship and the traits that characterize his own person and work.

Recall his admonition "whoever wishes to be great among you must be your servant, and whoever wishes to be first among you must be your slave" and the oft-cited symbolism of Jesus washing the feet of his disciples. "Jesus compares himself to one who serves at the table rather than one who sits and is served," writes Childs, and indeed there are many who believe that Jesus was executed not because he was this Messiah person but because he championed an egalitarianism that threatened the ruling elite.

This unlikely marriage of service and leadership has given rise to a contemporary theory of management called, not surprisingly, "servant-leadership." Its most passionate advocate was a man named Robert Greenleaf. Greenleaf was a management professional and student of leadership models who was profoundly moved by Hesse's story. It convinced him that the greatness of leaders is measured by the extent to which they truly serve others, and he founded an organization—The Greenleaf Center for Servant-Leadership—to further his ideas. In a seminal essay, "The Servant as Leader," he offered this definition of what makes a servant-leader:

> It begins with the natural feeling that one wants to serve, to serve first. Then conscious choice brings one to aspire to lead. . . . The difference manifests itself in the care taken by the servant—first to make sure that other people's highest priority needs are being served. The best test, and difficult to administer, is: do [those served] become healthier, wiser, freer, more autonomous, more likely themselves to become servants? *And*, what is the effect on the least privileged in society; will [they] benefit, or, at least, not be further deprived?

Greenleaf's emphasis on the value of leaders who put the needs of their employees, customers, and community above their own cannot be emphasized enough. This notion of service as a vital part of workplace meaning is gaining converts. Not a month goes by without a book on leadership coming out extolling the virtues of service to eager corporate managers looking for new motivational tools. Indeed, the servant-leadership model as a principle of enlightened management may be just on the cusp as a standard topic in academic business curricula. Craig Neal of the Heartland Institute, an organization devoted to bringing spirituality into the workplace, sees service as playing a pivotal role in how people perceive a more meaningful relationship to their work. "When people feel they are being of service to something larger than themselves, then something happens—an alchemy—that transcends logical thought and possibilities; the undoable gets done, the impossible is possible."

This is the kind of breakthrough thinking that is needed right now: seeing in our work the chance to serve, not just the person in front of us or on the other end of the phone, but the greater whole, which we are all a part of in countless ways. It is through this door that we can begin to find the inspiration to bring an entirely new attitude to our jobs. We aren't just getting a paycheck or filling time or performing our role as a dutiful member of society. We are actually in touch with the idea that we can have a *positive and meaningful* impact in the world.

I refer once more to the the wisdom of the East and the words of P. A. Payutto in *Buddhist Economics*:

> Buddhism makes a distinction between two kinds of happiness: dependent happiness and independent happiness. Dependent happiness . . . requires an external object. It includes any happiness contingent on the material world, including wealth, family, honor and fame . . . and leads to competition and conflict in the struggle to acquire material goods. Independent happiness, on the other hand, is the happiness that arises from within a mind that has been trained and has attained some degree of inner peace There is a third kind of happiness, [one] that is altruistically based, directed toward well-being and motivated by goodwill and

compassion. Through personal development, people can appreciate this truer kind of happiness—the desire to bring happiness to others.

5. Start the Day with Intention

Another way to unearth the meaning in our work is to create a daily ritual of affirmative intentions and stay alert to familiar traps of negativity or capitulation. The words of David Whyte in *Crossing the Unknown Sea* again seem appropriate to our mission: "In order to stand up against a force of nature, we often have to find that same elemental nature inside ourselves. Many times in our work lives we walk through the door with our shoulders hunched . . . feeling powerless and bullied." How different it would be to arrive at work in a state of mental and emotional preparedness.

Every morning begins as a blank page. What conversation with yourself do you usually start the day with? (It's been estimated that up to 90 percent of self-talk is negative.) What is your state of mind? Carpe diem? Grumbling dread? How can you create a new beginning to the workday that doesn't lead in the same old direction? As you stand in front of your mirror—hopefully after a cold splash of water or a wake-up rite of coffee or tea—take a moment and ask yourself some questions, for example, Is my heart open? Do I feel good about myself? How can I make a difference in the world? What do I want to achieve today? These are not easy questions. In fact, the commitment to change behaviors or beliefs will inevitably confront existing patterns of fear, self-identity and resistance. Change takes time, and even the most heartfelt intentions will travel a circuitous route.

"Intention is something waiting to be revealed, in layers," Cheryl Peppers and Alan Briskin write in *Bringing Your Soul to Work.*

> Our intentions are a mix of light and dark. By opening ourselves to the question of intention, we bring up from the bottom some of the darker elements that we need to understand as part of the

mix. We may start with our best intentions, such as service to others—then we get in touch with the more self-serving motivations of our need to dominate or be right. Honing our intentions, therefore, is an ongoing practice that goes deeper over time and in concert with our openness.

The point is that we can't get too complacent; affirming a positive change in outlook doesn't mean it happens overnight. And yet we don't have to leave home every day dressed in monkish garb, stone-faced with purpose. It just means moderating our expectations, cultivating a spirit of patience and self-awareness, and creating a space inside ourselves where new ways of thinking and feeling can start to grow. This process can start by ritualizing a commitment to specific and realistic intentions.

One way of doing this is to take a single day and turn it into an experiment. Decide to focus on one thing, say, detachment (not detachment that separates you from caring about what's happening but one that gives you permission to maintain some emotional distance). During this day, make a mental note of what is happening inside you or write down your impressions during private time in an "intention log." How does it feel to be in such a state? What are you learning? How are people responding to you? When you find yourself getting sucked in to old patterns, gently adjust your attitude. It will be difficult at times, especially when your particular buttons are being pushed, but that's okay. Look at the experience as exploratory research. At the end of the day, review what happened. Was there a noticeable difference in your experience? You can pick almost any quality that you aspire to—patience, enthusiasm, honesty, kindness, even joy—and try it on for a day. Practice them enough times and they start to become a part of you.

6. Find Moments of Solitude

One of the biggest obstacles to changing our experience at work is that the day rushes by so quickly that any new intentions can easily get swamped by the normal routines of acting and reacting that kick in as soon as we get there. Self-awareness? Beginner's mind? A spirit of service? The phone is ringing and the pile in my inbox is turning yellow! This is the reality; there will always be chaos at work, blows to our psyche, accumulating and conflicting demands on our time. Nevertheless, keeping that chaos from running our work lives is crucial to making room for a more meaningful relationship with our jobs.

Part of the answer, ironically, is slowing down. I don't mean drumming your fingers on the desk and staring out the window in a daydreamy mist, but making time, at work or elsewhere, for deep, focused reflection, to use however you feel you may need it. Solitude can help us quiet our mental chatter—the monkey mind—and sort things out without distraction, preparing for the next day's presentation or contemplating why a particular colleague seems troubled. Perhaps it's an opportunity to simply be silent with no particular agenda other than to shut out the noise. Peel off more layers and you may find yourself examining a deep loss of interest or a longing to see your work as something that matters.

In *Defining Moments*, Joseph Badaracco extols the value of solitude—what he calls "a space of quiet"—when the workplace confronts you with a thorny dilemma.

> The stakes are high: right-versus-right choices are defining moments in which managers reveal, test, and shape—sometimes irrevocably—their values and those of their organizations. These decisions involve difficult conflicts among managers' responsibilities to themselves, to other people in their organizations, and to other groups in society.

Inspired by the writings of the Roman emperor/philosopher Marcus Aurelius, he asks readers who find themselves in such ethical dilemmas to "work hard to create moments of serenity."

His message is relevant not just to mangers or in the face of a

specific moral challenge but to anyone who is trying to gain some lever-
age against a relentless work environment. I try to spend time every
day in a quiet space, sometimes pondering a specific issue and sometimes drifting into a more meditative state of longer and deeper stillness. I won't go on about the benefits such inner attention can
bring—they have long been championed by those in the East—but
skeptical Western minds will be pleased to know that laboratory data
is now validating the positive health impacts of regular meditation. In
fact, meditation is catching up to yoga as a legitimate stress-buster at
work. A recent article in *Business Week* online called "Zen and the Art
of Corporate Productivity" named a dozen companies where meditation has become standard corporate practice. This wave of enthusiasm
is apparently less a reflection of any spiritual revelation than recognition that stress costs money and meditation can help reduce it in a
cost-effective way. Whatever the motivation, it seems to work.

I'm less interested in solitude or meditation as tools for improving productivity, though, than as ways to keep us close to our inner
experience. Yes, better performance and more energy at work can be a
by-product, and that is not an insignificant result. More important is
what silence and self-reflection can reveal about the hidden patterns
at work in our emotions and our psyche. This is not the self-awareness
discussed in the previous chapter that entails active observation as we
go through our day, but a more intimate one-on-one where our deeper
thoughts and fears and intentions are available for review. It is here
that you may discover what's really keeping you from enjoying your
work. It is also the place to gauge your progress and to refresh your
mission with hope, keeping on the path even when it seems you've
gone as far as you can go.

The most powerful tool available for restoring meaning in the work we do is ourselves. We are largely in control of our experience; even in the most unpleasant situation we'll have choices in how to respond, each one leading to an outcome. Observing those outcomes and exploring the why behind the choices we make marks the beginning of workplace wisdom.

Andrew Ferguson, founder of an organization called Spirit in Business, recalled a conversation he had with the CEO of The Caux Round Table, an international group of senior executives who advocate "principled business leadership" and "ethical and responsible corporate behavior." "I learned," he reported, "that the sudden growth of Chief Ethics Officers in corporations has catalyzed a parallel need for employee personal growth—through mindfulness and spiritual practices . . . and that each individual must take personal responsibility for their own practice and actions in order for companies to act in a truly 'ethical' manner."

This challenge extends across the entire spectrum of work; no matter what your job is or how much responsibility you do or don't have, the battle to make work meaningful is ultimately a personal one, to be fought against our own conditioning to settle for less, to give in to the status quo, to sell our principles for cash. Overcoming our fears, taking risks, changing long-held attitudes, these are the keys to workplace transformation, whether or not our employers look ahead with similar vision. Paradoxically, as more and more people take their small steps toward healthier workplace consciousness, the organizations around them will change as well. As the process becomes reciprocal, then a true revolution will have started.

PART 5

conscious business

CHAPTER 11

The Whole-Self Workplace

The movement to bring spirit and soul to business is no passing fad; it continues to grow and with no signs of abating. Clearly, something significant and enduring is stirring the corporate world.
—PAUL WONG, President, International
Network on Personal Meaning

While the corporate responsibility movement continues to gain converts, another "movement" has been quietly bringing more meaning and purpose into the workplace: spirituality. Whether it's denominationally inspired, a deeply felt personal commitment, or a company-wide effort toward a values-driven mission, engaging directly with the challenges of work from a more soulful perspective is no longer considered off-limits. In fact, for growing numbers of both people and companies, such integration has become imperative as the instability and dehumanizing impacts of today's economic culture—both within our workplaces and without—provide less and less of what we need to feel whole. In such difficult times, it is no surprise that we're going beyond the surface realities of traditional business practice to find deeper sources of fulfillment and certainty.

Megatrends coauthor Patricia Aburdene contends that the next frontier of business will be predominantly spiritual in nature and predicts "a transformation of capitalism. The tenet of the Milton Friedman school that the sole purpose is to create economic value for shareholders is seen as having led us down the path to troubles, and this is compelling a rethinking of our philosophy of business."

The spirituality being discussed is largely seen less as a religious event and more as a desire to bring heart and values to how we conduct our jobs and our businesses. It has to do with how we stay balanced and find meaning in our work, how we treat others, how we handle adversity, how we face tough choices, and how our actions and policies impact the world we live in. It also includes the techniques we use to accomplish those things and the larger purpose we have for making such commitments in the first place, a purpose that usually transcends our own personal needs—but doesn't ignore them.

Judi Neal, a professor at the University of New Haven and founder of the Association for Spirit at Work, defines workplace spirituality as having both a horizontal and a vertical axis. "The vertical connects us with something greater, while the horizontal represents principles, values, and specific programs for nurturing the human spirit and making wise decisions." Some of those values include love, honor, service, integrity, kindness, respect, equality, ethics, community building, and stewardship. The challenge has been how to bring such qualities into the workplace, either as an individual practice or as part of wholesale organizational change.

An Explosion of Interest

This marriage of work and spirit isn't new, of course, but interest in the possibility took a quantum leap in the mid 1990s when a small group of pioneering writers and practitioners started talking out loud about it. That seemed to uncork a long-suppressed hunger for meaningful work, part of a broader awakening to the need to live a more spiritual life. The Princeton Religious Research Index, in a report delivered well *before* the traumatic impact of the September 11 terrorist attacks, found that religious beliefs and practices had increased sharply since the mid 1990s. When the Gallup Poll asked Americans in 1999 if they felt a need to experience spiritual growth, 78 percent said yes, compared to only 20 percent in 1994; nearly half said they'd talked about their faith in the workplace in the past twenty-four hours. Sales of Bibles and prayer books, inspirational volumes, and books about philosophy and Eastern religions kept pace and remain among the fastest-growing categories in publishing. Dozens of those titles have addressed spirituality at work.

There has also been an explosion of networking groups and events, both in the United States and throughout the world, which has brought thousands of diverse people together to explore just what is meant by spirituality and work. The longest running of these, the New Mexico-based International Conference on Business and Consciousness (formerly Spirituality and Business), held its ninth gathering in 2003 and featured such workshops as "Spiritual Economics: From the Marketplace to the Mountain," "Can Marketing Be Spiritual? Building Extraordinary Brands through the Power of Archetypes," and "The How-To of Business and Self: Points and Tips on Becoming Who You Really Are in the Business World."

A networking group called Spirit in Business, seeking to "enhance business performance and personal inspiration by integrating ethics, value and spirit in leadership and everyday business practice globally," has attracted companies from across the economic continuum. Among its nearly one hundred founding members were professionals from McDonalds, Phoenix Chemical Ltd., and The Rosicrucian Order. Strategic partners include The Conference Board and the Dalai Lama Foundation, while Forbes and Verizon Group were among the official sponsors of its inaugural "world conference" in 2002. More than five hundred people from more than thirty countries attended.

Such activity has not been lost on traditional business media. *Fortune* magazine made "God and Business" its July 2001 cover story.

In an article devoid of cynicism and snarky insinuations, it dealt respectfully with what once was a taboo subject in conservative business circles. After profiling a number of executives who have integrated spiritual practices into their work, it rightfully asked, "So what are we to make of this efflorescence of spirituality in the business world? Is this a superficial, merely utilitarian movement, or is it a genuinely spiritual awakening?" Its conclusion was surprising:

> We simply can't know whether today's ad hoc efforts to integrate faith and work will coalesce into something bigger and more powerful, with long-lasting effects, or whether they will fizzle. . . . In the end, though, it isn't likely that the faith-in-the-workplace movement will be driven by [bottom line pragmatism]. Nor will it be guided by consultants and churches. Rather, it will be powered, as it has been so far, by business people who yearn to find meaning in what they do. Whether there are enough of them, with sufficient will, to make a lasting difference remains to be seen, but they have begun talking, and that's a start.

Putting Principles and Values into Action

The first flush of excitement may have waned a bit since the idea of "spirituality and work" was put on the map nearly a decade ago, but the message has spread and spiritual principles, whether pursued individually or embraced company-wide, are popping up in a variety of places:

- Since 1993, more than twenty thousand executives from dozens of countries and blue chip multinationals have taken a forty-eight-hour course called Self-Managing Leadership (SML), developed by Brian Bacon and inspired by the principles of *raja yoga*, which advocate inner stillness through breath work, movement, meditation, and self-inquiry as the path to wisdom and inner balance.

- Exploring the convergence of East and West in the workplace is the aim of the Contemplative Net Project, which in late 2001 and early 2002 interviewed seventy-nine people who were incorporating contemplative practice into their work lives. The Project defines such ritual as, "A practice designed to quiet the mind in the midst of the stress and distraction of everyday life in order to cultivate a personal capacity for deep concentration and insight." It has developed a profile of what it calls the Contemplative Organization, characterized by efforts to:

  - Incorporate contemplative practices into all aspects of work
  - Embody its values
  - Move between cycles of action and reflection
  - Balance process with product
  - Have an organizational structure that reflects a contemplative philosophy

- Since 2002 the Willis Harman Spirit at Work Awards has honored a dozen companies "that have implemented specific policies, programs, or practices that explicitly nurture spirituality in their organizations." Harman was a futurist, social scientist, and writer whose life's work was helping people understand the role of consciousness in transforming business and society. Companies receiving the award have included a Minnesota-based medical manufacturer, a printing company in Canada, a London-based cosmetics chain, and a finance company in Calcutta.
- Typical of the work done by Harman award winners is The Methodist Hospital network in Houston. Several years ago the company hired a vice president of Spiritual Care to help the organization revitalize a mission that, in the words of the board, "had become too secular." It spent the next two years rewriting its key statements and then used a "cultural

assessment" tool to align its new core values —integrity, compassion, accountability, respect, and excellence—company-wide. The results so far, have been impressive:

- It has the highest patient satisfaction levels in its history.
- Helped in part by a creative recruitment effort, it now has the lowest nursing vacancy rate within the Texas Medical Center, considered one of the largest medical facilities in the world.
- The company was recently named one of the top 100 hospitals in the country by *U.S. News and World Report.*

- "Values-driven" management was also used to transform Unitel, a Canadian telecommunications company that became AT&T Canada, from a fading giant losing one million dollars a day into a financial success and one of the top five firms in North America in employee morale. The turnaround took less than five years. The values that their employees came up with—integrity, customer delight, respect for people, innovation, teamwork, and prudent risk-taking—might not appear to be overtly spiritual, but the focus on people and not profit behind the process represents a revolution in how organizations reinvent themselves.
- In 2001, the Australia & New Zealand Banking Group (ANZ) embarked on a radical new approach to improving productivity and employee moral. As reported by *wsj.com*, ANZ's "Breakout" program was originally designed to manage the impacts—primarily declines in employee and customer satisfaction—of a major reorganization that resulted in bank closures and job cuts. "Quiet rooms" were added to five of ANZ's seventeen business units and workshops created to, in the words of Sonia Stojanovic, head of the company's Cultural

Transformation Program, "help employees explore their own personal role in the company. We're trying to get out of the head and into the heart, to recognize first and foremost the humanity of colleagues and customers . . . .The basic question we ask people as part of this is, 'What does work mean to you?'" Approximately 10,000 of ANZ's 23,500 employees— primarily top executives and department heads—have taken the two- and three-day intensive personal-development courses. Since the program began, staff satisfaction levels have risen from 46 to 78 percent and the number of graduates applying for the 225 positions in the bank increased from 3,000 in 2001 to 11,000 in 2002.

Some of the efforts outlined above may be motivated in part by the persistent search for the "competitive edge" of a more productive workplace; companies being what they are and the market being what it is, such ambitions are understandable. As the *Forbes* article also reported, "Some believers claim that the core principles of spirituality—the belief that all individuals have dignity, that we are all interconnected, and that a transcendent being or force defines purpose in human affairs—dovetail with contemporary management thinking about what drives great companies."

At the same time, many of those at the forefront of this nexus of spirituality and work are struggling with their own personal challenges to overcome stress, make wise decisions, and balance their inner and outer lives. With transformational intent or not, they are open to change and willing to go outside the box for answers. The result: A remarkable variety of programs that are revolutionizing traditional management trainings. In both large and small ways, growing numbers of businesspeople are pushing the boundaries of what work is capable of encompassing.

New Ideas and Old Paradigms

As with any radical shift in perception that tries to swim in mainstream currents, introducing spiritual values at work has its challenges. Despite a growing number of success stories, not everyone is comfortable with mixing spirit—however defined—with work. "Even though you can show that those organizations with a spiritual orientation outperform others, even on the profit side, only a tiny percentage of business leaders 'get it,'" says Dr. Ian Mitroff, coauthor of *A Spiritual Audit of Corporate America*. "It's a different mind-set between reactive, bottom-line-driven organizations and those that are more humane, driven by higher values."

Even when a company makes such a commitment there are bound to be a few rough edges. As part of her doctoral thesis, professor of organizational communication Bethany Goodier shadowed the change-making efforts of Mount Carmel Health System in Columbus, Ohio, as it moved from a command-and-control model of management to "an avowedly spiritual" one. The process has been largely successful so far and certainly ongoing, she says, but it also created demands that put pressure on company resources. The time and energy needed to keep the process on track and top-of-mind are enormous. In addition, explains Goodier,

> [m]oney is needed for extra training and development and the various retreats that are used to do this. Then you have to pay others to do the work of those who are gone. There may also be new technologies required. The "language of love" that became part of the change process at Mount Carmel proved to be one of the biggest struggles for some employees.

Not everyone is comfortable opening themselves up in such an intimate way.

And yet the ultimate success of such efforts depends on broad employee involvement. The tools being used to facilitate these processes are thus designed to turn large groups of frequently disconnected people—personally as well as departmentally—into a nucleus of effective decision makers and advocates for change. One of the most popular of these, Open Space Technology (OST), was created in the mid 1980s by organizational consultant Harrison Owen. It is basically a self-organizing form of conferencing that relies on participants to come up with their own plan as they sit in a circle facing each other. The most important principle and prerequisite is that the people who show up be passionate about the topic and willing to take action on it. There are a few ground rules and guidelines, but most of what happens is in-the-moment, and what follows is a sometimes chaotic but always creative and forward-moving process in which community is created and objectives met. The track record of such processes as OST and Appreciative Inquiry (another open-ended model of community building and decision making) is impressive, but there will be bumps in the road as employees and executives are asked to stretch beyond their comfort zones, using communication tools that they aren't familiar with.

Once a "spiritual" or values-driven path is chosen, there can be unrealistic expectations of what will be achieved and when. I have seen numerous organizations and people with noble intentions fall prey to such very human weaknesses as ego, insecurity, overconfidence, and insensitivity to the worth and dignity of others. Of course, the drive for profits can have its own oppressive influence, although as business visionary Lance Secretan asserts, "The problem is not capitalism, it's how people treat each other." And so no matter how such foundational change is approached or what tools are used, progress, whether institutional or personal, is usually incremental and takes time. "There is a long learning curve," says Barbara Gordon of The Message Company, organizers of the Business and Consciousness gatherings, "from conceptual understanding of spiritual principles to successful real-life implementation. There are lots of great new ideas out there but too much reliance on old paradigm structures of execution." In short, there are no clear-cut models of how such a process works; the experience of each company and each individual in it will be different. Committed, enlightened, and patient leadership is thus vital to success.

Consultant Karen Wilhelm Buckley advises companies that want to integrate a more compelling spiritual ethic into their work environment to (1) "Point to ways in which work is already meaningful and to times when the organization's practices are demonstrating essential values," and (2) "Support all levels of management to make the common good the highest priority and to reflect this intention through *all dimensions of infrastructure*, including business processes, services, systems, work behaviors, culture and consciousness."

Spirituality with a small *s* is no longer something to be pursued and practiced outside of office walls; it is ready to become a vital component of our jobs, our careers, and perhaps even the companies we work for. Each of us will have our own reasons for making such a commitment, and the stress of our lives and the dysfunctions of our workplace will have played their part. But I believe that we're also being motivated by a deeper sense of personal calling, an innate imperative to more fully live out our noblest potential. As Daniel Taylor writes in *The Healing Power of Stories: Creating Yourself through the Stories of Your Life*, "Our greatest desire, greater even than the desire for happiness, is that our lives mean something. . . . Nothing makes us want to live more than the feeling that we have something important to do. Nothing makes us seem as worthless as the feeling that we do not."

And so we are being impelled by both interior and exterior forces to start remaking business and work into a force for positive change and personal renewal. Success will depend on our willingness to take risks, to be patient, and to stay connected to the larger vision of the vast potential before us. There is much to be done; the role we play is up to us. And whether we carry the mail or work in sales or head up a large division, there is potential for doing it better, more thoughtfully, more purposefully, and perhaps even more joyfully. Not to impress the boss or entice a raise or climb some corporate ladder, but because it is in those acts of conscious intention that we bring meaning back into what we do.

CHAPTER 12

Workplace Wisdom

I became more and more convinced that something great, something much greater than I had ever believed, is happening, and it is happening to all of us. We are indeed changing our beliefs. . . . The terrain (the systems on which we live) no longer corresponds with the map (our minds). The map is changing and the terrain must be adjusted accordingly.

— ROLF OSTERBERG, author of *Corporate Renaissance*

Rolf Osterberg was CEO of Scandinavia's largest film company, a former president of the Swedish Newspapers Association, and former chairman of numerous other companies. He is one of those corporate leaders who "converted" after a long and successful business career. Theologian and author Matthew Fox characterized his conversion as a "*metanoia* experience, wherein he questioned the direction [in which] his life in particular and work in general [were] evolving. He came to a point of realizing there must be more to work than the pure mechanics he was seeing." Osterberg is clearly not alone in this awakening; the "map" he refers to is changing for many of us. From isolated individuals applying spiritual principles to their labors to entire companies redefining their bottom line, there is growing evidence that a transformation is taking place.

Yet even as the need for workplace meaning touches more and more people's lives, counterbalancing forces of anxiety and fear grow

as well. We are living in a world of unprecedented change and institutional uncertainty, with an undertow of harsh reality that wants to
sabotage our good intentions. As the economic noose tightens and
global insecurity rises, time spent thinking about what work can
become competes with legitimate survival fears. Business as usual,
already a forbidding adversary, has for many become a much darker
place as relentless job cuts and executive avarice keep undermining
our trust; our work lives feel increasingly vulnerable as we scramble to
find safe harbor.

Survey after survey suggests a growing desperation for some level
of sanity, but the demands of everyday life seem to conspire against
us. Whitney Roberson, an Episcopalian minister at Grace Cathedral
in San Francisco, has spent years organizing and working with groups
of people who seek a deeper experience in their work. In the post-
911/post-Iraq era, however, she has sensed a falling back. "We are in societal trauma," she says. "Much of our energy is being used for coping."

Yes, the challenges we face at work are daunting, as this book has
readily admitted. The momentum of history, the tyranny of profit,
"jobless recoveries," and Darwinian notions of workplace and economic success, not to mention personal concerns over finances and
stress, can make the idea of meaningful work sound laughable, a quixotic
notion for starry-eyed idealists. And yet many of us have hit the wall;
we've reached the point where the work we do and the companies we
work for have failed to satisfy our need to feel connected and whole,
and we are starting to feel the loss. This discomfort is our souls nudg-
ing us to take action. Jean Kinkead Martine once lamented "in my
usual way of working I feel nothing precarious or risky. Nothing is
really at stake." We have now reached a point where everything is at
stake. If meaning is truly what we seek in our work, then we can no
longer act in isolation, either from the calling of our own deeper selves
or from the world around us within which we are intimately interconnected. Integration, compassion, wholeness, and relationship are

defining the new paradigm of business, and each incremental step we take in those directions will bring it closer to reality.

The Dawning of Extraordinary Business

At the 2003 meeting of the Academy of Management, the largest gathering of management scholars in the world (six thousand attendees), a new field of study was explored that according to reports generated more enthusiasm than any topic in recent memory. It goes by the awkward name of Positive Organizational Scholarship. POS represents a sea change in how to evaluate the process and goals of institutional renewal and transformation. It draws from the currently popular "positive psychology" movement that basically says that personal fulfillment is found not by obsessing on our problems and limitations but by identifying and then building on such moral strengths as valor, curiosity, perseverance, awe, and gratitude. The seminal, same-titled POS book that caused all of the buzz at the AOM conference "focuses attention on optimal *organizational* states—the dynamics in organizations that lead to the development of human strength, foster resiliency in employees, make healing, restoration, and reconciliation possible, and cultivate extraordinary individual and organizational performance." The first two paragraphs of the book are worth sharing because they offer a vivid portrait of just where these efforts may lead:

> Imagine a world in which almost all organizations are typified by greed, selfishness, competitiveness, manipulation, secrecy, dishonesty, and a single-minded focus on winning. Wealth creation is synonymous with success. Imagine that members of such organizations are characterized by distrust, anxiety, self-absorption, fear, burnout, and feelings of abuse. Conflict, lawsuits, contract breaking, retribution, and disrespect characterize many interactions and social relationships. Imagine also that scholarly researchers

investigating these organizations emphasize theories of problem solving, reciprocity and justice, managing uncertainty, overcoming resistance, achieving profitability, and competing successfully against others.

Now imagine another world in which almost all organizations are typified by appreciation, collaboration, peace, virtuousness, and human well-being. Creating abundance and vitality are key indicators of success. Imagine that members of such organizations are characterized by trustworthiness, resilience, wisdom, humility, generosity, and happiness. Social relationships and interactions are characterized by compassion, loyalty, honesty, love, respect, and forgiveness. Significant attention is given to what makes life worth living. Imagine that scholarly researchers emphasize theories of excellence, goodness, positive deviance, extraordinary performance, prospering, and positive spirals of flourishing.

Imagine, indeed! The fact that POS made such a strong impression on what probably is a rather conservative but influential group of academics is a profoundly optimistic sign. Leaders of business who are already following such principles don't ask if work was done as cheaply as possible and sold for the highest price but whether their companies are fulfilling their responsibilities as good corporate citizens and ethical employers and pushing the envelope of their humanitarian potential. Economic uncertainty and soulless capitalism may be all too real and prevalent, but a subculture of transformational business practice continues to mutate and grow, with plenty of inspirational examples of real commitment and change.

A Time for Personal Breakthrough

In this book I have often linked the institutional to the personal because in so many ways they are interwoven; our efforts to suffuse our work with meaning can be supported or sabotaged by the people and the companies we work for, while those very same efforts are crucial to corporate regeneration. This is true no matter what position or department one is in. Some of the challenges and opportunities will play out differently, of course, depending on your role—a CEO may contemplate mindfulness differently than, say, a software engineer, and responsibility for company-wide reform is often a top-down affair—but the search for meaning is an equal opportunity transformer. In fact, if you ask most people what's *really* important to them about a job or a company, many will name the same values, expectations, and goals. The problem is that something happens to those ideals somewhere between breakfast and when they park their car in the office lot. Certainly few of them survive by the end of a typical day.

In a sense, I'm advocating an approach to our work that emphasizes personal development and yet also goes beyond it, because ultimately we can't separate our work life from our nonwork life if meaning is what we're after, nor can we isolate our own well-being from that of the world we live in. The longing for fulfillment that follows us through the office door usually follows us out, and in both instances we are part of a larger whole. When I asked a dear friend of mine what kind of work she aspired to do, she said "My work, I've discovered, is not what I do as far as jobs go, but what I do internally. I 'work' on who I am and how I live. Where I do it is incidental." That may not be true for everyone, but what a powerful statement of personal responsibility and commitment.

I don't think that deep change can be pushed, though; even under the best of circumstances it takes time to rewire a belief system, and today those circumstances are as difficult as they have ever been for those who seek a better way. Not only must we overcome our own voices of resistance and fear but also those of the cultures in which we live and work. In a personal essay about the challenges to integrating spiritual values into our workplaces, business consultant Joan Marques wonders whether the West's predisposition toward individualism and competitiveness it too strong to overcome:

> Strategies to make progress in today's aggressive work environ-ment sometimes involve 'elbowing' the softer-hearted ones around us, and becoming close buddies with the ones we perceive as potential gateways to the top, even if we don't really like them. . . . [O]ur culture has taught us that this is justified. Only the strong survive.
>
> It is, after all, this very phenomenon called workplace politics that makes it unattractive for the well-intended ones among us to bring our entire "being" into work, since that would mean: providing openness about ourselves; exposing our most vulnera-ble sides, and, hence, allowing the sharks that oftentimes swim in the corporate ocean to take a huge bite in our souls.
>
> Therefore: if a spiritual workplace is one where we should be able to be our entire selves, we have to consider whether we should not change our cultural mindset first.

At the end of his demoralizing journey through the wreckage of Enron, Chris Seay wonders where the impetus for such a change will come from.

> Do we make new laws? Write new constitutions? Frame better ordinances? While some of that might help, it won't help much. Our problems will not be fixed by a new president, nor by a vig-ilant Securities and Exchange Commission, nor by a slew of leg-islation designed to infuse morality and decency into a population bubbling over with selfishness, escapism, and greed.
>
> Only a change of heart can do that.

The Dalai Lama emphasizes that such a shift can occur in any given moment, with each encounter we have, no matter how difficult a situation.

[I]n the workplace people may try to discover small things, small choices that they can make in how to go about their work. And of course, somebody may work on an assembly line with little variation in how to do their tasks, but they still have other kinds of choices in terms of their attitudes, how they interact with their co-workers, whether they utilize certain inner qualities or spiritual strengths to change their attitude at work even though the nature of the work may be difficult.

He acknowledges that injustice and exploitation must be actively resisted,

but at the same time we have to find ways to cope inwardly, ways to train our minds to remain calm and not develop frustration, hatred, or despair. That's the only solution. We may find help from our belief systems, whether we believe in karma or in God, but we can also use our human intelligence to analyze the situation and to see it from a different perspective.

What a powerfully clear expression of how each of us can reclaim some control over our work experience. Once we start using the tools at our disposal—mindfulness, detachment, intention, and the like— once we start "retraining our minds," an organic process unfolds and our thoughts and fears and assumptions and beliefs naturally re-form themselves over time. As we maintain our vigilance, keep track of our progress, and celebrate our triumphs, the changes become more tangible and permanent. I mentioned it before and I think it bears repeating: If the work we do doesn't feel meaningful, then the only option we have is to bring the meaning to it.

I do sense a fundamental shifting in the tectonic plates of our way of living, what David Korten has called "an epic cultural struggle . . .

a moment in time with deep implications not only for the future of humanity but also for life's evolutionary course." This struggle is showing itself in all of our major institutions, and certainly no less so in business. For it's not just a matter of making a job more interesting or a company more accountable, although these would be triumph enough; it's about evolving our work and our companies toward a higher order of consciousness.

I have imagined at great length how commerce could become a beautiful thing and lamented at equal length on how and why it isn't. I want to believe as Osterberg and Korten and others do that we are at the cusp of a grand economic transformation on both a personal and organizational level. I continue to deeply ponder the potential of corporate America to become a sustaining force for good, and of individual companies to become both thoughtful global citizens and places where our "whole selves," not just intellectual but also emotional and even spiritual, can be fully engaged. In Sweden, the oldest word for business—*naringsliv*—means "nourishment for life." In China the oldest symbols for business mean "life's meaning" or "life's work." The word *company* comes from the same root as *companion*. Perhaps the wisdom of the ancients is making itself known to us again. Is it unrealistic to harbor such hope, to believe that things can really be different? What will it take—individually, organizationally, and culturally—to transform the role of business and work in society and in our private lives? Those are the questions I have tried to answer in this book. All that's left is for each of us to keep doing the work.

Bibliography

Badaracco, Joseph L., Jr. *Defining Moments: When Managers Must Choose Between Right and Wrong.* Boston: Harvard Business School Press, 1997.

Badiner, Allan Hunt. *Mindfulness in the Marketplace: Compassionate Responses to Consumerism.* Berkeley, CA: Parallax Press, 2002.

Bakan, Joel. *The Corporation: The Pathological Pursuit of Profit and Power.* New York: Free Press, 2004.

Barrett, Richard. *Liberating the Corporate Soul: Building a Visionary Organization.* Cambridge: Butterworth-Heinemann, 1998.

Beder, Sharon. *Selling the Work Ethic: From Puritan Pulpit to Corporate PR.* London: Zed Books, 2000.

Berenson, Alex. *The Number: How the Drive for Quarterly Earnings Corrupted Wall Street and Corporate America.* New York: Random House, 2003.

Berger, Peter L. *Homeless Mind: Modernization and Consciousness.* New York: Vintage, 1974.

Cameron, Kim S., Jane E. Dutton, and Robert E. Quinn. *Positive Organizational Scholarship: Foundations of a New Discipline.* San Francisco: Berrett-Koehler, 2003.

Cherniss, Cary and Daniel Goleman, eds. *The Emotionally Intelligent Workplace: How to Select For, Measure, and Improve Emotional Intelligence in Individuals, Groups, and Organizations.* San Francisco: Jossey-Bass, 2001.

Childs, James M. Jr. *Ethics in Business: Faith at Work.* Minneapolis: Augsburg Fortress, 1995.

Collins, Jim. *Good to Great: Why Some Companies Make the Leap . . . and Others Don't!* New York: HarperCollins, 2001.

Collins, Jim and Jerry Porras. *Built to Last: Successful Habits of Visionary Companies.* New York: HarperBusiness, 1994.

Cutler, Howard, and His Holiness the Dalai Lama. *The Art of Happiness at Work*. New York: Riverhead Books, 2003.

Dalla Costa, John. *The Ethical Imperative: Why Moral Leadership Is Good Business*. New York: Perseus Publishing, 1998.

Davidson, Let. *Wisdom at Work: The Awakening of Consciousness in the Workplace*. Burdett, NY: Larson Publications, 1998.

Easwaran, Eknath. *Ghandi the Man: The Story of His Transformation*. Tomales, CA: Nilgiri Press, 1997.

Eisenberger, Robert. *Blue Monday: The Loss of the Work Ethic in America*. St. Paul, MN: Paragon House, 1989.

Estes, Ralph W. *Tyranny of the Bottom Line: Why Corporations Make Good People Do Bad Things*. San Francisco: Berrett-Koehler, 1996.

Fenichell, Stephen and Jeffrey Hollender. *What Matters Most: How a Small Group of Pioneers Is Teaching Social Responsibility to Big Business, and Why Big Business Is Listening*. New York: Basic Books, 2003.

Fox, Matthew. *The Reinvention of Work: A New Vision of Livelihood for Our Time*. New York: HarperSanFrancisco, 1994.

Furnham, Adrian. *The Protestant Work Ethic: The Psychology of Work-Related Beliefs and Behaviours*. London: Routledge, 1990.

Giroux, Henry. *Impure Acts: The Practical Politics of Cultural Studies*. New York: Routledge, 2000.

Greider, William. *The Soul of Capitalism: Opening Paths to a Moral Economy*. New York: Simon & Schuster, 2003.

Harman, Willis, and John Hormann. *Creative Work: The Constructive Role of Business in Transforming Society*. N.p.: Knowledge Systems, 1991.

Hartmann, Thom. *Unequal Protection: The Rise of Corporate Dominance and the Theft of Human Rights*. Emmaus, PA: Rodale Press, 2002.

Hertz, Noreena. *The Silent Takeover: Global Capitalism and the Death of Democracy*. New York: Free Press, 2002.

Hochschild, Arlie. *The Time Bind: When Work Becomes Home and Home Becomes Work*. New York: Metropolitan Books, 1997.

Huffington, Arianna. *Pigs at the Trough: How Corporate Greed and Political Corruption Are Undermining America*. New York: Crown, 2003.

Izzo, John, and Pam Withers. *Values Shift: The New Work Ethic and What It Means for Business*. Gloucester, MA: Fairwinds Press, 2001.

Jennings, Kate. *Moral Hazard: A Novel*. London: Fourth Estate, 2002.

Kelly, Marjorie. *The Divine Right of Capital: Dethroning the Corporate Aristocracy*. San Francisco: Berrett-Koehler, 2001.

Korten, David C. *The Post-Corporate World: Life after Capitalism*. San Francisco: Berrett-Koehler, 2001.

———. *When Corporations Rule the World*. San Francisco: Berrett-Koehler, 2001.

Leider, Richard. *The Power of Purpose: Creating Meaning in Your Life and Your Work*. San Francisco: Berrett-Kohler, 1997.

Mitroff, Ian, and Elizabeth A. Denton. *A Spiritual Audit of Corporate America: A Hard Look at Spirituality, Religion, and Values in the Workplace*. San Francisco: Jossey-Bass, 1999.

Paine, Lynn Sharp. *Value Shift: Why Companies Must Merge Social and Financial Imperatives to Achieve Superior Performance*. New York: McGraw-Hill, 2003.

Payutto, P. A. *Buddhist Economics: A Middle Way for the Marketplace*. Badger, CA: Torchlight Publishing, 1996.

Peppers, Cheryl, and Alan Briskin. *Bringing Your Soul to Work: An Everyday Practice*. San Francisco: Berrett-Koehler, 2000.

Phillips, Kevin. *Wealth and Democracy: A Political History of the American Rich*. New York: Broadway Books, 2002.

Richards, Dick. *Artful Work: Awakening Joy, Meaning, and Commitment in the Workplace*. San Francisco: Berret-Kohler, 1995.

Ritz, Dean. *Defying Corporations, Defining Democracy: A Book of History and Strategies*. New York: Apex Press, 2001.

Schor, Juliet B. *The Overspent American: Why We Want What We Don't Need*. New York: Basic Books, 1998.

————. *The Overworked American: The Unexpected Decline of Leisure.* New York: Basic Books, 1992.

Schroth, Richard J., and A. Larry Elliott. *How Companies Lie: Why Enron Is Just the Tip of the Iceberg.* New York: Crown Business, 2002.

Seay, Chris, and Christopher Bryan. *The Tao of Enron: Spiritual Lessons from a Fortune 500 Fallout.* Colorado Springs, CO: Navpress, 2002.

Sinetar, Marsha. *Do What You Love, the Money Will Follow.* Mawah, NJ: Paulist Press, 1987.

Spears, Larry C., and Michele Lawrence (editors). *Practicing Servant Leadership: Succeeding through Trust, Bravery, and Forgiveness.* San Francisco: Jossey-Bass, 2004.

Tapscott, Don and David Ticoll. *The Naked Corporation: How the Age of Transparency Will Revolutionize Business.* New York: Free Press, 2003.

Terkel, Studs. *Working.* New York: Ballantine, 1985.

Tulku, Tarthang. *Mastering Successful Work.* Berkeley: Dharma Publishing, 1994.

Waugh, Barbara, Margot Silk Forrest, and Alan Webber. *The Soul in the Computer: The Story of a Corporate Revolutionary.* Makawao, HI: Inner Ocean Publishing, 2001.

Whyte, David. *Crossing the Unknown Sea: Work as a Pilgrimage of Identity.* New York: Riverhead Books, 2001.

————. *The Heart Aroused: Poetry and the Preservation of the Soul in Corporate America.* New York: Doubleday, 1994.

Wilkinson, Bruce, and Howard Hendricks. *The Prayer of Jabez: Breaking Through to the Blessed Life.* Sisters, OR: Multnomah Publishers, 2000.

Woodruff, Paul. *Reverence: Renewing a Forgotten Virtue.* New York: Oxford University Press, 2002.

About the Author

Matthew Gilbert was the editor of a publishing trade magazine for six years and has been a facilitator and consultant for many small companies. He has written extensively on business, psychology, and spirituality and is the author of *Communication Miracles at Work* and *Take This Job and Love It*. Gilbert is now the editor-in-chief of *Shift: At the Frontiers of Consciousness*, published by the Institute of Noetic Science. He lives in California with his wife and their two cats.

to our readers

Conari Press, an imprint of Red Wheel/Weiser, publishes books on topics ranging from spirituality, personal growth, and relationships to women's issues, parenting, and social issues. Our mission is to publish quality books that will make a difference in people's lives—how we feel about ourselves and how we relate to one another. We value integrity, compassion, and receptivity, both in the books we publish and in the way we do business.

Our readers are our most important resource, and we value your input, suggestions, and ideas about what you would like to see published. Please feel free to contact us, to request our latest book catalog, or to be added to our mailing list.

Conari Press
An imprint of Red Wheel/Weiser, LLC
P.O. Box 612
York Beach, ME 03910-0612
www.conari.com